BROUGHT TO YOU BY:

SUPERKID ACADEMY
A SIMPLE GUIDE FOR HOME USE

MY FATHER LOVES ME

BIBLE STUDY FOR KIDS!

Ordinary kids doing extraordinary things through the power of God's Word!

ISBN 978-1-60463-327-6   30-1069

Superkid Academy Home Bible Study for Kids—My Father Loves Me

© 2010 Eagle Mountain International Church Inc. aka Kenneth Copeland Ministries

Kenneth Copeland Publications
Fort Worth, TX 76192-0001

For more information about Kenneth Copeland Ministries, call 1-800-600-7395 (U.S. only) or +1-817-852-6000 or visit kcm.org.

SuperkidAcademy.com • 1-800-606-4190

TABLE OF CONTENTS

WELCOME!

Dear Parent/Teacher,

I believe you will experience great and exciting things as you begin the faith adventure of *Superkid Academy Home Bible Study for Kids—My Father Loves Me.*

As you launch into this faith-building time with your family or small group, take the opportunity to seek the Lord's direction about how to minister these lessons for maximum impact. God's Word does not return to Him void, and He will see to it that your children are BLESSED and grow strong in faith as you step out in His Anointing to teach them about Him.

Please keep in mind that we are praying for you. We believe and release our faith for a powerful anointing on you as you teach and impart His wisdom, and that your Superkids are strong in the Lord and mighty for Him.

Remember, we here at Academy Headquarters want to be a resource for you. Make sure you are in our contact base so we can keep in touch. And, let us know how we can better serve you and your Superkids.

We love you and look forward to hearing from you!

Love,

Commander Kellie

Commander Kellie

LEADING YOUR SUPERKID ACADEMY:
A SIMPLE GUIDE FOR HOME USE

We are excited that you have brought Superkid Academy into your living room with the Home Bible Study for Kids! This powerful, Bible-based curriculum will guide your children into building a strong, personal relationship with the Lord and inspire them to live an extraordinary, faith-filled life.

Each of the 13 weeks included in this study provide five days of lessons, including a:

- **Lesson Introduction From Commander Kellie:** As the creator of Superkid Academy with more than 20 years' experience ministering to children, Kellie Copeland has a unique anointing and perspective for reaching children with the uncompromised Word of God. She passes on her wisdom through these timeless segments.
- **Lesson Outline:** Each lesson contains three main points, subpoints and supporting scriptures to empower you to clearly communicate the truth to your children.
- **Memory Verse:** Throughout the week, your kids will have the opportunity to memorize and understand a scripture. More than that, they'll learn how to apply it directly to their lives.
- **Bible Lesson:** Each Bible Lesson reinforces the memory verse and the principle behind it. Discussion questions will help you lead your children through not only comprehending the passage of scripture, but also giving it meaning in their lives.
- **Giving Lesson:** Each week, you will have the opportunity to teach your children about the importance of tithing and giving so they can be "blessed to be a blessing" in the Body of Christ.
- **Game Time:** Reinforces the message and gives families an occasion to celebrate what they've learned in a fun way.
- **Activity Page:** Reinforces the lesson through acrostics, word searches, mazes and other puzzles.
- **Supplements:** Support the memory verse and lesson—two will be provided each week, including:
    - **Object Lesson:** Illustrates the focus of the lesson and provides visual and hands-on elements to the teaching.
    - **Real Deal:** Highlights a historical person, place or event that illustrates the current lesson's theme.
    - **Read-Aloud Stories and You-Solve-It Mysteries:** Reinforces the message with creative, read-aloud stories.
    - **Food Fun:** Takes you and your children into the kitchen where you will discuss, illustrate and experience God's truth, using everyday items.
    - **Academy Lab:** Brings the lesson and science together.

And, don't forget the enclosed Praise and Worship CD! These original, upbeat, kid-friendly songs put the Word in your children's minds and hearts. The CD can be listened to around the house or in the car, and the karaoke, sing-along tracks allow your kids to sing their favorite songs.

Making the Curriculum Work for Your Family

Superkid Academy's Home Bible Study for Kids gives you the flexibility to teach your children in a way that works for you. Each week's lesson is divided into five days of teaching. However, we understand that no two families—or their schedules—are the same, so feel free to adjust the lessons to meet your needs. Use all five days of lessons or select only a few to cover each week. Whether you're using the curriculum as part of your home school, as a boost to your family devotions or in a weekly small group, you have the flexibility to make it work for you.

A Homeschool Bible Curriculum

Superkid Academy's Home Bible Study for Kids is easy to use, flexible and interactive—no dry Bible lessons here! It is ideal for a variety of learning styles. Each of the 13 weeks contains five days of lessons—one Bible Lesson, one Giving Lesson, one Game Time and two other lessons or stories to support the week's message. You may choose to use all five days of lessons or pick and choose the ones that work best for your educational structure. Optional variations for several of the lessons have been included to meet a variety of needs.

Each week's Snapshot provides the major points of the lesson, the memory verse and a list of supplies needed for that week, allowing you to easily prepare and customize each week's lessons. Here are just a few additional ideas for customizing for your home school:

- Re-read the Bible passage each day throughout the week to give your children—and you—time to meditate on the high-lighted scripture
- Use one or more of the discussion questions as a journaling exercise
- Begin a weekly, family Game Night
- Use the Storybook Theater in your nighttime read-aloud routine

Family Devotions

Superkid Academy's Home Bible Study for Kids empowers you to disciple your children and teach them the Word of God in an easy, fun way. You may choose to use all five days' worth of lessons, or select only a few. Each lesson takes less than 15 minutes, so the curriculum fits easily into your busy life.

Lessons are numbered 1-5, giving you the flexibility to include whichever lesson fits your daily schedule for that week. This allows you freedom to plan around work schedules, church commitments and extracurricular activities. Here are two sample schedules:

5-Day Schedule

Sunday—Church (no lesson)

Monday—Bible Lesson

Tuesday—Object Lesson

Wednesday—Midweek services (no lesson)

Thursday—Giving Lesson

Friday—Storybook Theater

Saturday—Game Time

3-Day Schedule

Sunday—Church (no lesson)

Monday— Bible Lesson

Tuesday—Soccer practice (no lesson)

Wednesday—Giving Lesson

Thursday—Soccer practice (no lesson)

Friday—Object Lesson

Saturday—Family time (no lesson)

A Weekly Small Group

Superkid Academy's Home Bible Study for Kids is designed for use over several days, but a week's worth of lessons can easily be consolidated for a small group. Simply choose the lessons that work best for your location and schedule and allow additional time for discussion and prayer.

Sample Small Group Schedule:

6 p.m.	Bible Lesson with discussion time
6:30 p.m.	Giving Lesson
6:45 p.m.	Object Lesson and prayer time
7:15 p.m.	Game Time
7:45 p.m.	Refreshments
8 p.m.	Closing

Thank you again for implementing Superkid Academy's Home Bible Study for Kids. We stand with you in faith as you disciple your children in the things that matter to Him. Proverbs 22:6 *(KJV)* says, "Train up a child in the way he should go: and when he is old, he will not depart from it." At Superkid Academy, we are confident that God will bless your efforts, and that you and your children will see the reality of THE BLESSING in all you do (Numbers 6:24-26).

Love,

Commander Kellie

Commander Kellie

HEALTH & SAFETY DISCLAIMER FOR "SUPERKID ACADEMY CURRICULUM"

Superkid Academy is a ministry of Eagle Mountain International Church, aka Kenneth Copeland Ministries (hereafter "EMIC"). The "Superkid Academy Curriculum" (hereafter "SKA Curriculum") provides age-appropriate teaching material to be used in the religious instruction of children. The SKA Curriculum includes physical activities in which children and leaders may participate. Before engaging in any of the physical activities, participants should be in good physical condition as determined by their health care provider. EMIC is not responsible for injuries resulting from the implementation of activities suggested within the SKA Curriculum. Prior to implementing the SKA Curriculum, carefully review your organization's safety and health policies, and determine whether the SKA Curriculum is appropriate for your organization's intended use.

By purchasing the SKA Curriculum, I, individually and/or as authorized representative for my organization, hereby agree to release, defend, hold harmless, and covenant not to sue EMIC, its officers, deacons, ministers, directors, employees, volunteers, contractors, staff, affiliates, agents and attorneys (collectively, the "EMIC Parties"), and the property of EMIC for any claim, including claims for negligence and gross negligence of any one or more of the EMIC Parties, arising out of my use or organization's use of and participation in the SKA Curriculum, participation in the suggested activities contained within the SKA Curriculum, or resulting from first-aid treatment or services rendered as a result of or in connection with the activities or participation in the activities.

WEEK 1: THREE IN ONE

 Memory Verse: *So there are three witnesses in heaven: the Father, the Word and the Holy Spirit, and these three are One.* —1 John 5:7 AMPC

WEEK 1: SNAPSHOT — THREE IN ONE

DAY	TYPE OF LESSON	LESSON TITLE	SUPPLIES
Day 1	Bible Lesson	Jesus' Baptism	None
Day 2	Real Deal	Freeze-Drying	1 Astronaut action figure or picture of an astronaut, 1 Bag of freeze-dried ice cream or other freeze-dried food samples
Day 3	Giving Lesson	Let Go of That Seed!	Package of seeds, Watering can, Flashlight, Clay pot, Potting soil, Small table
Day 4	Object Lesson	It's All Here	2 Hard-boiled eggs (or 1 egg for each child), Kitchen table, Paper towels, Plastic gloves
Day 5	Game Time	Triathlon	Punch ball, Jump-rope, Hula hoop, Stopwatch, Watch with second hand or smartphone with stopwatch app, Upbeat music to play during the activity (optional)
Bonus	Activity Page	Trinity Match-Up	1 Copy per child

Lesson Introduction:

When teaching a challenging subject like the Trinity, it's important to allow input and questions from your kids. It's a good challenge to the Cadets to process what they are learning and explore ways to incorporate its truth into their everyday lives.

Choosing to provide examples in more than one form and expressing the different expressions of that element may be a helpful tool in relating to the Trinity (or the main point of each lesson). Here are two examples:

- Water can appear in three different states—liquid (water), gas (steam) or solid (ice).
- Words can be thought, spoken or written.

God is unique. He is Three in One—the Father, the Son, and the Holy Spirit!

Love,

Commander Dana

Commander Dana

Lesson Outline:

This week, your children will learn about the Trinity, the marvelous mystery of God's presence. You will help them understand that although God appears in three different persons—the Father, the Son and the Holy Spirit—He is still one God.

Enjoy sharing this foundational truth with your children this week. Explore how God, in three persons, works together. Answer their questions about the function of each person of the Trinity. Encourage discussion, and look for ways to impart this truth throughout the week.

I. AN AMAZING MYSTERY SOLVED

a. God is three persons in One. 1 John 5:7

b. Our God is Father, Son and Holy Spirit.

c. The Trinity is in unity and agreement. 1 John 5:8

II. GOD'S WISDOM IS REVEALED TO US BY HIS SPIRIT
1 Corinthians 2:14

a. We are to seek wisdom and understanding from God. Proverbs 4:7

b. We walk in wisdom when we follow God's Word. Matthew 11:19

c. We seek the Spirit of wisdom to know God better. Ephesians 1:17

III. THE TRINITY

a. God is our heavenly Father, and the Creator of all. Genesis 1:1

b. Jesus is our Savior, our friend, and our way to God. John 14:6

c. The Holy Spirit is our helper. Romans 8:26

Notes: _____

_____

_____

_____

_____

_____

_____

_____

DAY 1: BIBLE LESSON | **JESUS' BAPTISM**

Memory Verse: *So there are three witnesses in heaven: the Father, the Word and the Holy Spirit, and these three are One.* —1 John 5:7 AMPC

This week, we're learning about the Trinity—that God is Three in One. In this passage about Jesus' baptism, we see the Godhead—the Father, the Son and the Holy Spirit—working together in perfect unity, preparing the way for Jesus' ministry, death and resurrection, and God's redemption of mankind.

Read Matthew 3:13-17:
The Baptism of Jesus

Then Jesus went from Galilee to the Jordan River to be baptized by John. But John tried to talk him out of it. "I am the one who needs to be baptized by you," he said, "so why are you coming to me?"

But Jesus said, "It should be done, for we must carry out all that God requires." So John agreed to baptize him.

After his baptism, as Jesus came up out of the water, the heavens were opened and he saw the Spirit of God descending like a dove and settling on him. And a voice from heaven said, "This is my dearly loved Son, who brings me great joy."

Discussion Questions:

1. **What happened in this passage?**

   John the Baptist baptized Jesus. When that happened, the Holy Spirit descended on Jesus and God spoke.

2. **All three persons of the Godhead—the Father, the Son and the Holy Spirit—were present at this moment in time. Identify each one in this passage.**

   Jesus was being baptized. The Holy Spirit descended from heaven like a dove, and the Father was the voice from heaven.

3. **Jesus' baptism was the beginning of His ministry on earth. Why was this important?**

   From this point until His death and resurrection, Jesus began teaching people about His heavenly Father. Many people came to know Him and accept Him as their Lord. He was the fulfillment of God's promise to save mankind.

4. **Why was it important for all three persons of the Godhead to be present at that point in history?**

   Jesus' baptism was an important part of God's plan for mankind's redemption, and all three persons of the God-head had a part in its success. As we already learned, Jesus' baptism was the beginning of His ministry and part of His journey toward crucifixion (paying for all of mankind's sins) and resurrection (overcoming death). It was through these key events that we are in right-standing with God and can have a relationship with Him. Surely, none of the Godhead—Father, Son or Holy Spirit—would have wanted to miss this eternal event!

Notes: _____

_____

_____

_____

_____

_____

_____

_____

_____

_____

_____

_____

_____

_____

_____

_____

_____

_____

_____

_____

_____

_____

_____

_____

_____

DAY 2: REAL DEAL

FREEZE-DRYING

 Memory Verse: *So there are three witnesses in heaven: the Father, the Word and the Holy Spirit, and these three are One.* —1 John 5:7 AMPC

 Concept: Highlighting an interesting historical place, figure or event that illustrates the theme of the day. The theme of the day is Three in One—God present in God the Father, God the Son, and God the Holy Spirit.

Supplies: ☐ 1 Astronaut action figure or picture of an astronaut, ☐ 1 Bag of freeze-dried ice cream or other freeze-dried food samples (available at most outdoor stores or camping sections in department stores)

Intro:

Today we're talking about amazing mysteries. In fact, we're talking about one of the greatest mysteries of all time—the Trinity. The Trinity refers to the Godhead, or God as three people in One—Father, Son and Holy Spirit. Sounds amazing, doesn't it?

Today, we're going to look at something else that remains the same, even when it changes form. But first, let's see if you can answer this riddle:

"We started traveling in the 1960s. Our trips were very long—to say the least. They were so long, in fact, that we needed a lot of food to eat. Who are we?"

Any guesses? *(Reread the riddle, and maybe give some hints. Allow children to guess.)*

The answer is: astronauts!

What Is It?

This week, we're learning about astronauts. Can someone tell me our Bible memory verse again? So, what does that have to do with astronauts? Well, let's find out!

When astronauts travel into space, they still have to eat! But they can't take regular food with them like we eat, because they have to have food that doesn't need to be kept in the refrigerator or that takes up much space. A space capsule or cabin where the astronauts ride is very compact, so there's no place to store as much regular food as a crew would need on a long journey like that.

So, scientists had to figure out how to bring along food that would be easy to pack, ready to eat and took up very little space.

Scientists decided to send along *freeze-dried* food. I think you're probably wondering what that is! Well, when food is freeze-dried, it weighs a lot less because once the moisture is taken out, it shrinks in size and lasts for a long time. Some space food can last up to 30 years! Wow, now that's amazing!

How Do They Do That?

I'm sure you're probably wondering how food is freeze-dried. Let's find out!

Freeze-drying food takes three steps. First, scientists invented a freeze-drying machine that freezes food at 50-80 degrees below zero. Now, that's cold! Just think, it only has to be 32 degrees *above* zero to snow or make ice cubes.

After the freeze-drying machine freezes the food, a high-powered vacuum sucks out all the ice crystals that have formed inside the food after it has been frozen at such cold temperatures. This process leaves little holes in the food where the ice crystals were, creating something like a sponge out of the food. Then the food is heated until it completely dries out. And now, the food is finally ready to put into flat, airtight packages so it can last a long time and fit into the small space where the astronauts will ride.

The first American astronauts had shorter trips into space, and didn't require as much food. This was a good thing because early space food wasn't too appetizing. The early freeze-dried foods were a big step, but they needed some work to make them better. They were usually in liquid form that the astronauts sucked out of aluminum tubes. It was a challenge to keep the tubes from crumbling. And, speaking of crumbs, if the astronauts ate anything that left crumbs, if they weren't watchful, the crumbs would float away and get into their equipment. Not good!

The NASA scientists worked on the freeze-dried food until they were eventually able to freeze-dry meals that actually tasted homemade. Astronauts were able to enjoy meals that many people like, like lasagna, shrimp, chicken, vegetables and even ice cream!

(Allow your children to see, smell and taste the freeze-dried food that has been rehydrated.)

Let's Eat!

So, how is freeze-dried food prepared? The main component in it is water. As we learned, the water is taken out of the food in the form of ice crystals, to make it last longer and be lighter to transport. But to make it edible, or to "bring it back to life," water needs to be added back into it. In the early days, the astronauts had to use their saliva to bring freeze-dried food back to life. Yuck! That meant no hot meals, just cold dinners every night—not much fun.

Eventually, NASA scientists created a device that carried hot water into space for the astronauts to be able to prepare warm meals. Even though using the hot water to prepare the freeze-dried meals took longer—about 20-30 minutes per meal—no one was complaining! The astronauts couldn't have been happier about having hot meals for their long journeys into space.

Today's space-shuttle menus contain about 72 different foods and 20 different kinds of drinks.

Making History:

Did you know that freeze-drying food has been around for more than 1,000 years? The ancient Inca Indians in Peru were the first people to freeze-dry food using the high altitudes and extreme mountain temperatures where they lived. In the winter months, they would store their crops in the cold and return in summer to find them perfectly unspoiled. They used nature as their natural freeze-dryer!

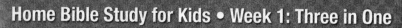

Today, freeze-dried food is the meal of choice for many hikers and campers because it's light to carry and takes up very little space in a backpack.

Outro:

There are so many interesting mysteries in the world. While freeze-dried food is interesting, and it's fun to find out about how things work, it doesn't even compare to the wonderful mystery of the Trinity—God the Father, God the Son and God the Holy Spirit. Today's Real Deal really opens our eyes to see how something can look and act differently but still be essentially the same. God the Father, God the Son and God the Holy Spirit may operate differently in our lives, but they're still the same God!

Notes: _____

_____

_____

_____

_____

_____

_____

_____

_____

_____

_____

_____

_____

_____

_____

_____

_____

_____

_____

_____

_____

_____

_____

DAY 3: GIVING LESSON

LET GO OF THAT SEED!

Suggested Time: 10 minutes

Offering Scripture: There are those who [generously] scatter abroad, and yet increase more; there are those who withhold more than is fitting or what is justly due, but it results only in want.
—Proverbs 11:24 AMPC

Parent Tip: This is a perfect opportunity to express the importance of a generous and willing attitude. Remind and encourage your children to be generous givers with their time and service. This is also an excellent lesson to perform outside.

Supplies: ☐ Package of seeds, ☐ Watering can, ☐ Flashlight, ☐ Clay pot, ☐ Potting soil, ☐ Small table

Prior to Lesson:

Be sure to communicate to your children the concept of sowing generously into God's kingdom. It is only by giving from our hearts—our money, time and talent—that we can receive a harvest.

Lesson Instructions:

Today, we're going to talk about Proverbs 11:24. It says, "There are those who [generously] scatter abroad, and yet increase more; there are those who withhold more than is fitting..." [more than they should].

Let's discover what this means. First, I'm going to need a Superkid who doesn't mind getting dirty to help me. I need a helper who loves to dig in the dirt, likes to work in the garden, and enjoys seeing things grow. *(Choose a Superkid to be your helper.)* Right here, on this table, is everything needed to grow a plant: a seed, a clay pot, some dirt, water and sunlight *(hold up your flashlight)*. Well, it's almost like sunlight! Let's go ahead and do what is needed to plant this seed. *(Allow one of your children to place soil in the clay pot and prepare to water the seed. Hold the seed up for everyone to see, and keep it clenched in your hand, making sure they realize the seed is in your hand.)*

Now that we have everything prepared, it's time to water and give sunlight to our seed. *(Keeping the seed in your hand, review the planting steps. Make sure the children recognize that the seed is still in your hand. Once the kids notice that the seed is missing from the clay pot, place the seed in the pot, have fun with the flashlight—sunlight.)*

Did you know that this example of the seed relates to today's scripture? It points out that people who are not generous givers end up with just more needs. For example, instead of planting a seed, a stingy person wants to continue holding on to the seed while he/she is still expecting a harvest. But that's not the way it works. To receive any harvest, like fruits and vegetables, we must plant a seed. We must let go of the seed so we can plant it in the ground.

So let's be generous people with our money, our things and our talents by "planting our seeds," and giving to those in need. When we do, we're sure to end up with *more* joy and goodness in our lives.

Let's prepare our offering for this week's church service!

Variation No. 1: Garden

Instead of conducting this lesson inside, you may choose to do it in your garden or flower bed.

Variation No. 2: Giving Box

Challenge the children to fill an empty box with toys, clothes and canned goods to donate to those in need. In addition to filling the box, allow them to be part of delivering the box to the charity of their choice—Goodwill, a local food pantry, a shelter, etc.

Notes: _____

_____

_____

_____

_____

_____

_____

_____

_____

_____

_____

_____

_____

_____

_____

_____

_____

_____

_____

_____

_____

DAY 4: OBJECT LESSON | IT'S ALL HERE

Suggested Time: 10 minutes

Memory Verse: *So there are three witnesses in heaven: the Father, the Word and the Holy Spirit, and these three are One.* —1 John 5:7 AMPC

Supplies: ■ 2 Hard-boiled eggs (Only one egg is required for the lesson. Keep one for a backup, or if you would like each child to participate, include 1 egg for each.), ■ Kitchen table, ■ Paper towels, ■ Plastic gloves (for your child to wear while holding the egg)

Lesson Instructions:

Hey, Superkids, do you know what's in my hand? *(Hold up one of the eggs.)* Yes, it's an egg. That was an easy question, wasn't it?

Well, here's a more challenging question: Can one of you Superkids describe the different parts of an egg? *(Allow children to name the different parts: shell, white and yolk.)* Just to make sure, we're going to take this egg apart to find all three parts.

As you can see, I'm taking off the outside part of the egg. What is this called? You're right! The outside part of the egg is called the shell. *(If each child has an egg, instruct children to crack the shell and start peeling their eggs.)* To reveal the egg white, we'll have to remove all the shell.

Ta da! Presenting…the egg white! So now, there's only one part left. Let's reveal the final part. Can anyone remember what the third part is called? Yes, it's the yolk. *(Help children carefully remove the white to expose the yolk of the egg.)* Here it is, right in the middle. Now, this egg has been separated into three parts, which all came from the one egg.

You know, that so reminds me of God! God is just one God, but He has three parts—just like this egg. There is the Holy Spirit, whom we'll compare to the shell of the egg. The Bible says the Holy Spirit hovers around us, which means He "hangs out" over us. Then, there's the Son of God, Jesus, who is like this egg white because He's right next to the Father, who is the center of everything, just like this yolk. Isn't that cool—to be three parts, put together, to make one! And just like this egg, there's always more of God than can be seen with our natural eye!

Notes: _____

_____

_____

_____

_____

_____

DAY 5: GAME TIME

TRIATHLON

 Suggested Time: 8-10 minutes

 Memory Verse: So there are three witnesses in heaven: the Father, the Word and the Holy Spirit, and these three are One. —1 John 5:7 AMPC

 Teacher Tip: Present the memory verse to your children and allow them to repeat it several times. Include your own hand gestures and movements to help them memorize it more easily.

Supplies: ☐ Punch ball, ☐ Jump-rope, ☐ Hula hoop, ☐ Stopwatch, watch with second hand or smartphone with stopwatch app, ☐ Upbeat music to play during the activity (optional)

Prior to Game:

Begin by blowing up and tying the punch ball. Set up 3 stations around the yard or house, 1 for each activity.

Game Instructions:

Today, we're going to play a really fun game. Who likes to jump rope? How about using a hula hoop? What about punch balls?

Is anyone good at all three? But, what about at the same time? *(Choose 1 player to attempt all 3 activities at the same time.)* Oh, my! It's not so easy to do them all at the same time, is it?

Well today, we're going to have a triathlon. Does anyone know what that is? A *triathlon* is an athletic contest with three consecutive events, usually swimming, bicycling and distance running. But, instead of those three events, we're going to jump rope, hula-hoop and hit punch balls!

We'll have three stations. At each station, a player will do each event, and when he/she has completed the number of times required, he/she can move on to the next station. *(Choose the order in which players will move through the stations.)*

When I say, "Go!" the player will rush to the punch-ball station, pick it up and punch it 10 times. When the player finishes all 10 times, he/she will move to the hula-hoop station where he/she will hula-hoop 10 times. Finally, the player will run to the jump-rope station where he/she will jump rope 10 times. The winner will be the player with the fastest times.

Game Goal:

Be the player to move through all 3 stations the fastest. The player with the fastest time, wins!

Final Word:

It was very challenging to attempt to do all three activities at one time. What's amazing about the Trinity is that God the Father, Jesus and the Holy Spirit work together, all at the same time!

Variation No. 1: Parent Play

Parents, don't miss this opportunity to play with your children. Become one of the participants and make a meaningful memory as well as a powerful lesson.

Variation No. 2: Beat Yourself

For children with different skill levels, have them play against themselves. Time each run to determine if each person can beat his/her own time.

Notes: _____

_____

_____

_____

_____

_____

_____

_____

_____

_____

_____

_____

_____

_____

_____

_____

_____

_____

_____

_____

ACTIVITY PAGE **TRINITY MATCH-UP**

 Memory Verse: *So there are three witnesses in heaven: the Father, the Word and the Holy Spirit, and these three are One.* —1 John 5:7 AMPC

ANSWER KEY:

PSALM 68:5: FATHER TO THE FATHERLESS, DEFENDER OF WIDOWS— THIS IS GOD, WHOSE DWELLING IS HOLY.

JOHN 8:58: JESUS ANSWERED, "I TELL YOU THE TRUTH, BEFORE ABRAHAM WAS EVEN BORN, I AM!"

ROMANS 8:26: AND THE **HOLY SPIRIT** HELPS US IN OUR WEAKNESS. FOR EXAMPLE, WE DON'T KNOW WHAT GOD WANTS US TO PRAY FOR. BUT THE HOLY SPIRIT PRAYS FOR US WITH GROANINGS THAT CANNOT BE EXPRESSED IN WORDS.

I CORINTHIANS 8:6A: BUT FOR US, THERE IS ONE GOD, THE **FATHER**, BY WHOM ALL THINGS WERE CREATED, AND FOR WHOM WE LIVE.

FATHER

JOHN 14:26: BUT WHEN THE FATHER SENDS THE ADVOCATE AS MY REPRESENTATIVE—THAT IS, THE **HOLY SPIRIT** —HE WILL TEACH YOU EVERYTHING AND WILL REMIND YOU OF EVERYTHING I HAVE TOLD YOU.

I CORINTHIANS 8:6B: AND THERE IS ONE LORD, **JESUS CHRIST**, THROUGH WHOM ALL THINGS WERE CREATED, AND THROUGH WHOM WE LIVE.

JOHN 3:16: FOR THIS IS HOW **GOD** LOVED THE WORLD: HE GAVE HIS ONE AND ONLY SON, SO THAT EVERYONE WHO BELIEVES IN HIM WILL NOT PERISH BUT HAVE ETERNAL LIFE.

JESUS

JOHN 14:17: HE IS THE **HOLY SPIRIT**, WHO LEADS INTO ALL TRUTH. THE WORLD CANNOT RECEIVE HIM, BECAUSE IT ISN'T LOOKING FOR HIM AND DOESN'T RECOGNIZE HIM. BUT YOU KNOW HIM, BECAUSE HE LIVES WITH YOU NOW AND LATER WILL BE IN YOU.

ISAIAH 9:6: FOR A CHILD IS BORN TO US, A **SON** IS GIVEN TO US. THE GOVERNMENT WILL REST ON HIS SHOULDERS. AND HE WILL BE CALLED: WONDERFUL COUNSELOR, MIGHTY GOD, EVERLASTING FATHER, PRINCE OF PEACE.

HOLY SPIRIT

I JOHN 5:20: AND WE KNOW THAT THE **SON OF GOD** HAS COME, AND HE HAS GIVEN US UNDERSTANDING SO THAT WE CAN KNOW THE TRUE GOD. AND NOW WE LIVE IN FELLOWSHIP WITH THE TRUE GOD BECAUSE WE LIVE IN FELLOWSHIP WITH HIS SON, JESUS CHRIST. HE IS THE ONLY TRUE GOD, AND HE IS ETERNAL LIFE.

JOHN 14:6: JESUS TOLD HIM, "I AM THE WAY, THE TRUTH, AND THE LIFE. NO ONE CAN COME TO THE FATHER EXCEPT THROUGH ME."

Name:_____

Throughout this week, you've learned that God is Three in One, one God as three different people—the Father, the Son and the Holy Spirit. Look up the verses below, fill in the missing words and match each to the correct person of the Godhead. (Note: All scriptures have been taken from the *New Living Translation*.)

PSALM 68:5: _____ TO THE FATHERLESS, DEFENDER OF WIDOWS—THIS IS GOD, WHOSE DWELLING IS HOLY.

JOHN 8:58: _____ ANSWERED, "I TELL YOU THE TRUTH, BEFORE ABRAHAM WAS EVEN BORN, I AM!"

ROMANS 8:26: AND THE _____ _____ HELPS US IN OUR WEAKNESS. FOR EXAMPLE, WE DON'T KNOW WHAT GOD WANTS US TO PRAY FOR. BUT THE HOLY SPIRIT PRAYS FOR US WITH GROANINGS THAT CANNOT BE EXPRESSED IN WORDS.

I CORINTHIANS 8:6A: BUT FOR US, THERE IS ONE GOD, THE _____, BY WHOM ALL THINGS WERE CREATED, AND FOR WHOM WE LIVE.

FATHER

JOHN 14:26: BUT WHEN THE FATHER SENDS THE ADVOCATE AS MY REPRESENTATIVE—THAT IS, THE _____ _____ —HE WILL TEACH YOU EVERYTHING AND WILL REMIND YOU OF EVERYTHING I HAVE TOLD YOU.

I CORINTHIANS 8:6B: AND THERE IS ONE LORD, _____ _____,THROUGH WHOM ALL THINGS WERE CREATED, AND THROUGH WHOM WE LIVE.

JOHN 3:16: FOR THIS IS HOW _____ LOVED THE WORLD: HE GAVE HIS ONE AND ONLY SON, SO THAT EVERYONE WHO BELIEVES IN HIM WILL NOT PERISH BUT HAVE ETERNAL LIFE.

JOHN 14:17: HE IS THE _____ _____, WHO LEADS INTO ALL TRUTH. THE WORLD CANNOT RECEIVE HIM, BECAUSE IT ISN'T LOOKING FOR HIM AND DOESN'T RECOGNIZE HIM. BUT YOU KNOW HIM, BECAUSE HE LIVES WITH YOU NOW AND LATER WILL BE IN YOU.

ISAIAH 9:6: FOR A CHILD IS BORN TO US, A _____ IS GIVEN TO US. THE GOVERNMENT WILL REST ON HIS SHOULDERS. AND HE WILL BE CALLED: WONDERFUL COUNSELOR, MIGHTY GOD, EVERLASTING FATHER, PRINCE OF PEACE.

I JOHN 5:20: AND WE KNOW THAT THE _____ _ _____ HAS COME, AND HE HAS GIVEN US UNDERSTANDING SO THAT WE CAN KNOW THE TRUE GOD. AND NOW WE LIVE IN FELLOWSHIP WITH THE TRUE GOD BECAUSE WE LIVE IN FELLOWSHIP WITH HIS SON, JESUS CHRIST. HE IS THE ONLY TRUE GOD, AND HE IS ETERNAL LIFE.

JOHN 14:6: _____ TOLD HIM, "I AM THE WAY, THE TRUTH, AND THE LIFE. NO ONE CAN COME TO THE FATHER EXCEPT THROUGH ME."

Notes: _____

_____

_____

_____

_____

_____

_____

_____

_____

_____

_____

_____

_____

_____

_____

_____

_____

_____

_____

_____

_____

_____

_____

_____

_____

_____

_____

_____

WEEK 2: THE ULTIMATE FATHER

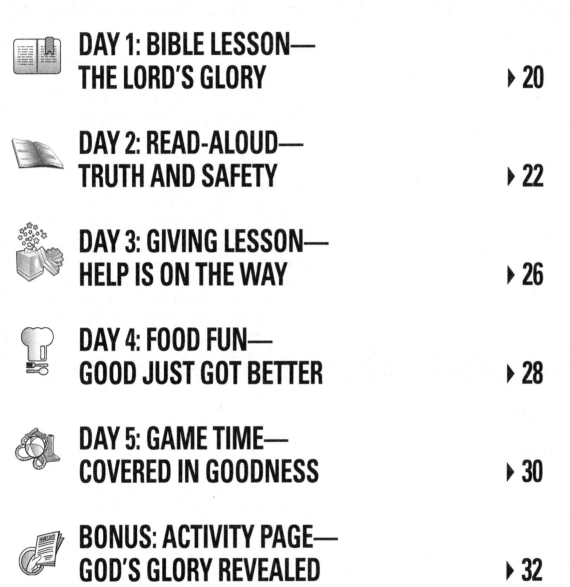
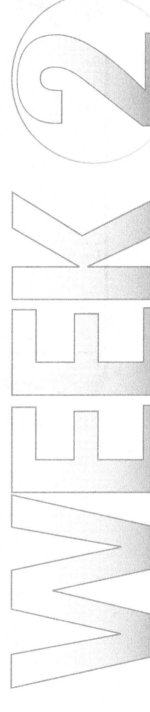

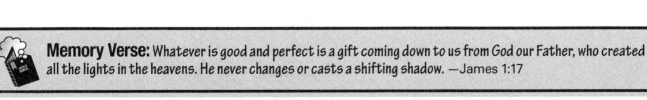

Memory Verse: *Whatever is good and perfect is a gift coming down to us from God our Father, who created all the lights in the heavens. He never changes or casts a shifting shadow.* —James 1:17

WEEK 2 SNAPSHOT — THE ULTIMATE FATHER

DAY	TYPE OF LESSON	LESSON TITLE	SUPPLIES
Day 1	Bible Lesson	The Lord's Glory	None
Day 2	Read-Aloud	Truth and Safety	Optional Props: Baseball mitt, ball and hat
Day 3	Giving Lesson	Help Is on the Way	5-Gallon bucket (filled with water) or water hose with sprayer attachment, 1 Pitcher, 1 Large pail
Day 4	Food Fun	Good Just Got Better	1 Medium-sized mixing bowl, 1 Extension cord or power supply, 1 Electric hand mixer, Measuring cups, Measuring spoons, Serving spoons, Plastic spoons, 2 Aprons, 8-Ounce carton heavy whipping cream, 2 Tablespoons sugar, 1 Teaspoon vanilla, 1/4-1/2 Cup chocolate drink powder (Ex: Nesquik®)
Day 5	Game Time	Covered in Goodness	2 Pairs of goggles, Shaving cream or whipped cream, 2 Bags of colored miniature marshmallows, Paper towels and/or baby wipes, Small fun (non-food) prizes or rewards, Stopwatch, Stopwatch app on a smartphone or watch with a second hand, Upbeat music (optional)
Bonus	Activity Page	God's Glory Revealed	1 Copy for each child

Lesson Introduction:

When teaching about God, it's important to consider your children's examples. Children tend to view God through a lens that is influenced by the adults in their lives. Perhaps your children's father has been a strong, positive and faithful role model. Or maybe he's been emotionally or physically absent from their lives, or worse. This can have an effect on their perception of what God is like, especially when we refer to Him as "Heavenly Father." Either way, before you begin this lesson, it's important to pray about how to communicate God's goodness to your children in a way that will speak to them. Ask the Holy Spirit to lead you in sharing the truth about God's goodness in a way that will resonate in their hearts. I like to tell children that God is the only perfect Father, the only one who has never made a mistake or done the wrong thing.

Throughout the week, invite your children to ask questions about God, His goodness and what a friendship with Him looks like. Remember this; *Your relationship with God might be the greatest influence for them.* Your ultimate goal in this lesson is to communicate this truth: "God is the ultimate Father, and when we ask Him to be our Lord, our Savior *and our Father,* we are welcomed into the greatest family in the world!"

Love,

Commander Dana

Commander Dana

Lesson Outline:

This week, you'll have the opportunity to teach your children about God, the Father. They'll learn about His wondrous works and His loving nature. Enjoy introducing your children to their heavenly Father in a deeper way.

I. GOD, THE FATHER, IS GENEROUS

a. God created this world for us to enjoy. Genesis 1:26

b. God gave His only Son, Jesus, to offer us eternal life. John 3:16

c. God wants His children to put their hope in Him and enjoy His gifts in their lives. 1 Timothy 6:17

II. GOD, THE FATHER, IS OUR PROTECTOR

a. The children of Israel encountered dangerous enemies. 2 Chronicles 20

b. When God's children ask for help, He listens! 2 Chronicles 20:7-24

c. Our Father is bigger than the world's father! 1 John 4:4

III. GOD, THE FATHER, IS GOOD

a. God is good, and God is love. Matthew 19:17

b. God showed Moses His goodness. Exodus 33:19

c. God is patient, kind and merciful. Romans 2:4

Notes: _____

_____

_____

_____

_____

_____

_____

_____

_____

_____

_____

_____

DAY 1: BIBLE LESSON — THE LORD'S GLORY

Memory Verse: Whatever is good and perfect is a gift coming down to us from God our Father, who created all the lights in the heavens. He never changes or casts a shifting shadow. —James 1:17

God, the Father, is kind and loving. He bestows good and perfect gifts on His children, and as the memory verse reminds us, He never changes. Ask the Holy Spirit to reveal God's glory and goodness to you in even greater measure today so that you can, in turn, communicate it to your children.

Read Exodus 33:12-23:
Moses Sees the Lord's Glory

One day Moses said to the Lord, "You have been telling me, 'Take these people up to the Promised Land.' But you haven't told me whom you will send with me. You have told me, 'I know you by name, and I look favorably on you.' If it is true that you look favorably on me, let me know your ways so I may understand you more fully and continue to enjoy your favor. And remember that this nation is your very own people."

The Lord replied, "I will personally go with you, Moses, and I will give you rest—everything will be fine for you."

Then Moses said, "If you don't personally go with us, don't make us leave this place. How will anyone know that you look favorably on me—on me and on your people—if you don't go with us? For your presence among us sets your people and me apart from all other people on the earth."

The Lord replied to Moses, "I will indeed do what you have asked, for I look favorably on you, and I know you by name."

Moses responded, "Then show me your glorious presence."

The Lord replied, "I will make all my goodness pass before you, and I will call out my name, Yahweh, before you. For I will show mercy to anyone I choose, and I will show compassion to anyone I choose. But you may not look directly at my face, for no one may see me and live." The Lord continued, "Look, stand near me on this rock. As my glorious presence passes by, I will hide you in the crevice of the rock and cover you with my hand until I have passed by. Then I will remove my hand and let you see me from behind. But my face will not be seen."

Discussion Questions:

1. **What did Moses want God to do?**

   Moses wanted God to reveal who He was going to send along with Moses as Moses led the children of Israel to the Promised Land.

2. **Who did God say would go with Moses and the children of Israel?**

   God Himself promised to go with Moses.

3. **What did Moses say would happen if God did, indeed, go with the children of Israel?**

Moses said, "Your presence among us sets your people and me apart from all other people on the earth."

4. **What did Moses mean by that statement?**

Nothing else can compete with God's presence. Moses knew that if God was with them, then the children of Israel would be protected and blessed.

5. **Then, what did Moses ask God to do?**

He asked to see God's presence.

6. **Did God do as Moses asked? If so, what happened?**

Yes, God did as Moses asked. He had Moses stand by a rock and covered him with His hand as He walked by. Moses only saw God's back, not His face.

7. **Why couldn't Moses look at God's face?**

God's presence was too great and powerful for Moses, or any man or woman, to look at. No human in a flesh body can see God's face and live.

8. **What do we learn about God from this passage?**

Parents, there are several themes to explore with your children:

- God's glorious presence
- God's promise to stay with us, His people
- God's mercy and compassion, which He shows to us, His people
- God's willingness to communicate with us and answer our questions
- God's protection, even when the danger is unknown to us.

Notes: _____

_____

_____

_____

_____

_____

_____

_____

_____

_____

_____

DAY 2: READ-ALOUD   TRUTH AND SAFETY

Suggested Time: 15 minutes

Memory Verse: Whatever is good and perfect is a gift coming down to us from God our Father, who created all the lights in the heavens. He never changes or casts a shifting shadow. —James 1:17

Optional Props: ☐ Baseball mitt, ball and hat (as props or to hold and wear as you tell the story)

Background:

Today, your children will meet two childhood friends who are involved in a tough situation with a bully at school. Perhaps at the end of the story, you can discuss the bullying issue with your children and their experiences, or yours. Emphasize that God is our protector, and when we trust Him to help us, He is there to deliver in every situation.

Peter's lie to his parents was not a wise choice—even though the situation seemed dire enough to him to temporarily justify his untruthfulness. Discuss the importance of telling the truth.

Story:

Peter and his friend Alex squared off against each other, wearing their mitts and throwing the baseball back and forth. Like most recent afternoons, they were practicing in the street of their cul-de-sac, testing out different kinds of throws—fastballs, sliders and grounders.

Usually, they had to wait until Peter finished his math homework to practice but, well, not today. Peter cringed inwardly remembering the lie he had told his mother. He hadn't meant to lie, but he had carelessly forgotten his math book in his dad's car the day before, so he couldn't finish his homework. And, he couldn't *not* practice. Not today. Too much was at stake, what with the school bully Frankie Calloway hounding Peter and Alex mercilessly, telling the whole world what losers they were. Hopefully, his parents would understand.

"You think we're ready for tomorrow's game?" Alex asked, pulling Peter back to the present.

The two had been inseparable since moving into the neighborhood when they were 5. From kindergarten on, they had wrestled, played hide-and-go-seek and even dodged the occasional Frisbee® thrown at them by Frankie.

"I hope so," Peter said, lobbing another grounder Alex's way. "I don't even want to think about what it will mean if Frankie's team beats us."

"That's the truth."

Eyeing Peter's father's car turn down the street, the boys moved out of the way to let him pass. The car slowly turned into the driveway and parked in the garage.

Peter ran over to him. "Hey Dad, we still on for throwing the ball today? I want to practice before the big game tomorrow. Remember, this one's important. We *have* to win."

His dad chuckled, "Well, good afternoon to you, too." He grabbed Peter in a playful headlock and then released him. "Yes, we can play catch. Let me just change and say hello to your mother."

Peter ran back to Alex. "My dad's coming out in just a few minutes. He'll help us get ready for tomorrow."

Before long, Peter's dad came outside and slowly walked toward Peter, his face creased in a frown that Peter had seen before.

"Peter, did you finish your math homework?" Peter's dad asked, his gaze intense.

"Sure, Dad, all done." Peter's eyes darted to the ground. Butterflies formed in his stomach.

His dad paused before asking, "How is that possible when your math book was in my car? You forgot it in there after I picked you up from school yesterday."

"Uh…well…I meant that…I was going to do it as soon as you came home, right after dinner." He held his breath as he waited for his father's reaction.

"No, that's not what you said. You told your mother and me that you'd already finished your homework. That was a lie."

It sounded so ugly coming from his father's mouth. *A lie.* The one thing his father had clearly and repeatedly told him not to do. Peter shifted his weight from one foot to the next. He wanted to go back 20 minutes to when his father had just returned home. No, he wanted to go back even further to the moment he had told his mother the lie. Maybe even *further,* back to the moment when he had forgotten his math book in his father's car in the first place. Yes, that was the moment he wanted to relive. That was the moment when everything was good and normal and right.

Finally, Peter's shoulders dropped and his eyes rested on the ground at his father's feet. "I lied. I wanted to come outside and play ball with Alex. I knew if Mom knew I hadn't finished my homework, she wouldn't allow me to do it. And this game is *really* important."

"You know the rules. No playing with friends until your homework is finished."

"Yes, sir."

"I know this game is important, but lying is never excusable," his father continued.

"Yes, sir."

"Look at me, son." Peter slowly raised his eyes to his father's.

"You can always tell me the truth. You can trust me, and I need to know that I can trust you. Understand?"

"Yes, sir."

"You want to tell me why this game is more important than the others? Why is it so important that you would lie to me and your mom about it?"

Peter looked over at Alex and then back at his dad. Could he admit the humiliation of sharing what was really happening with Frankie at school? Would his dad understand just how miserable it would be if their team lost and Frankie could lord it over them for the rest of their lives?

Nervously, Peter shifted back and forth. "It's Frankie."

"Frankie Calloway? You guys are friends."

"No, Dad, we used to be friends, but that was a long time ago." Slowly, Peter began telling him all about Frankie's antics. He told his dad about Frankie tripping him on the school bus and stealing Alex's backpack only to throw it out the bus' window into a nearby mud puddle. He told him about Frankie embarrassing him and Alex in the hallways at school and calling them names. Before long, Alex joined the conversation and together the boys shared the embarrassing and painful experiences they had been living.

Peter's dad asked a few questions but mostly, he just listened. When Peter and Alex had finally finished, Peter's dad put an arm around each boy.

"Sounds like it's been pretty miserable."

Peter and Alex readily agreed. "Yeah, it's been bad."

"Well, I'm glad you told me about it. You boys shouldn't have to put up with a bully like that. I know Frankie's dad. He and I will be having a talk."

Then he turned to Peter. "You know this is no excuse for lying to me and your mom though, right?"

"Yes, sir."

"Good. Tomorrow, after the game, I expect you to do some extra chores as a consequence, and to help remind you that lying is *never* OK."

"Yes, sir."

"But, I also understand that you've felt pretty desperate because of this situation with Frankie. I can help you with that now that you've told me."

Peter smiled at his dad, allowing his dad to pull him into a hug.

Then, his dad turned to Peter's friend and patted him on the back. "Alex, I'm going to have you go home now because Peter has some math homework to do."

Alex smiled big. "Thanks, Mr. Newton."

Peter waved goodbye to his friend and walked into the house with his dad. He was certainly thankful he had confided in his dad and that his dad was on his side. Knowing that, regardless of what happened at the game the next day, he couldn't possibly lose.

Discussion Questions:

1. **What happened in the story?**

   Answers will vary, but make sure your children understand the story.

2. **How did Peter's father respond to his son's lie?**

   He was disappointed. He told Peter, "You can always tell me the truth. You can trust me, and I need to know that I can trust you."

3. **How did Peter's father respond when he found out about Frankie's behavior toward Peter and Alex?**

   He planned to talk to Frankie's father.

4. **Do you think our heavenly Father responds to us in a similar way when we make mistakes?**

   Yes, God the Father is disappointed when we sin. He wants us to trust and love Him enough to follow His ways.

5. **Do you think our heavenly Father wants to protect us?**

   Absolutely. He protects His kids. Of course, He needs us to listen to Him and His Word so that we make good choices.

Notes: _____

_____

_____

_____

_____

_____

_____

_____

_____

_____

_____

_____

_____

_____

_____

_____

_____

_____

_____

_____

_____

_____

_____

DAY 3: GIVING LESSON   **HELP IS ON THE WAY**

 Suggested Time: 10 minutes

 Offering Scripture: So let us come boldly to the throne of our gracious God. There we will receive his mercy, and we will find grace to help us when we need it most. –Hebrews 4:16

 Parent Tip: This offering lesson will focus on help coming just when we need it. Emphasize the focus on *help* in this scripture so your kids can easily understand the main theme of this lesson activity.

Supplies: ■ 5-Gallon bucket (filled with water) or water hose with sprayer attachment, ■ 1 Pitcher (to hold and pour water), ■ 1 Large pail

Prior to Lesson:

Teach this lesson outside. Fill the 5-gallon bucket with water or have a water hose ready to fill a pitcher at regular intervals.

Lesson Goal:

The goal of this activity is to demonstrate the importance of asking God for help, and trusting Him to help us each day. The strong child, holding the pail, will be challenged by the increased water weight and begin to falter, and eventually call out for help.

Lesson Instructions:

Who would like to help me with this lesson? I'm going to need a really strong person to hold this pail. *(Choose a strong child to hold the pail. Another child will fill the pitcher with water from the 5-gallon bucket or water hose and slowly pour water into the pail.)*

So, how many pitchers of water in this bucket do you think you can hold? *(Address the child holding the bucket, and allow other children or family members to count out loud as each pitcherful is added. If your child chooses to not ask for help, the water will eventually spill. Continue this activity until your child chooses to ask for help or the water spills. Let your children know you were willing to help all along, they just needed to ask! Have fun with this activity and remind your children that it's OK to ask for help when situations are challenging.)*

When you got tired of holding the heavy pail, all you needed to do was ask for help, and I was ready to step in! It's the same with God. He's always ready to step in and help us whenever we need it. All we need to do is ask!

Let's read our scripture for today from Hebrews 4:16 together: "So let us come boldly to the throne of our gracious God. There we will receive his mercy, and we will find grace to help us when we need it most."

Let's honor God and His goodness by preparing our offering for this week's service.

Variation: One Child

If you have only one child, allow him/her to hold the bucket while you pour in the water. Let your Superkid instruct you as to when to pour the water so that they are in control of how much water is added.

Notes: _____

_____

_____

_____

_____

_____

_____

_____

_____

_____

_____

_____

_____

_____

_____

_____

_____

_____

_____

_____

_____

_____

_____

_____

_____

_____

DAY 4: FOOD FUN

GOOD JUST GOT BETTER

Suggested Time: 10 minutes

Memory Verse: Whatever is good and perfect is a gift coming down to us from God our Father, who created all the lights in the heavens. He never changes or casts a shifting shadow. —James 1:17

Parent Tip: Read the recipe and the lesson in their entirety before you begin. You will assemble the recipe while you are sharing the lesson.

Recipe:

Ingredients: ☐ 8-Ounce carton heavy whipping cream, ☐ 2 Tablespoons sugar, ☐ 1 Teaspoon vanilla, ☐ 1/4-1/2 Cup chocolate drink powder (Ex: Nesquik®)

1. Pour whipping cream into mixing bowl and beat with hand mixer on high speed, gradually adding sugar as cream begins to thicken.
2. Stir in vanilla.
3. Add chocolate drink powder to desired "chocolaty-ness."

Supplies: ☐ 1 Medium-sized mixing bowl, ☐ 1 Extension cord or power supply, ☐ 1 Electric hand mixer, ☐ Measuring cups, ☐ Measuring spoons, ☐ Serving spoons, ☐ Plastic spoons, ☐ 2 Aprons

Lesson Instructions:

Welcome to today's Food Fun! We're going to make a really yummy treat. Who'd like to help me with this recipe? *(Begin preparing the recipe. Start by pouring the whipping cream into the bowl.)*

Mmmm, I can already taste how yummy it's going to be! *(Once the whipping cream is in the bowl, turn the mixer on high and blend until it begins to thicken. Remove the mixer and allow your helper to continue stirring the whipping cream with a spoon while you share the passage from Luke 18:18-22.)*

God's Word tells us about a young man who asked Jesus what "good" thing he needed to do to attain eternal life. This young man had kept all God's commandments since he was a little boy, but there was still something missing in his heart.

Have you already heard this story? *(This is a great time to allow the kids to share and discuss this story while having one of your children add the sugar to the whipping cream. Use the mixer to combine the ingredients. After mixing the whipping cream and sugar, have your assistant add the vanilla. Use the mixer to combine the three ingredients. The whipping cream should be getting close to being ready.)*

Now for the last touch, we'll add the secret ingredient! *(Have fun playing up the secret ingredient. Stir in the chocolate and blend with the mixer.)*

You know, adding all the special ingredients to this recipe is like the story of the young man who asked Jesus what "good" thing he could do to attain eternal life. He wanted to know what other "special" ingredient he was missing in his heart. Jesus told the young man to sell what he owned, give to the poor, and follow after Him. Jesus wanted the young man to know that there is only One who is good and perfect—God—not the things he owned or how many people he knew or what family he came from. And, Jesus also wanted him to know that if he would sow into others, like to the poor, God would bless him with so much more: good measure, pressed down, shaken together and running over! (See Luke 6:38.)

This story is like our recipe. The whipped cream was good by itself, but after adding the sugar, the vanilla and the chocolate, it kept getting better and better with each ingredient.

Choosing to add more of God's "special ingredients" to our daily lives (like His love, His peace, His joy, etc.) will help us live lives that are pleasing to Him and a blessing to others. And, He will make sure that when we bless others, He will bless us with way more in return!

Variation: Non-Dairy Option

If your children have a dairy allergy, substitute full-fat, canned coconut cream for the whipping cream. If you can't find coconut cream in your grocery, simply purchase a can of coconut milk (make sure it is full-fat and does not contain guar gum). Refrigerate the can upside down overnight. When you're ready to present the lesson, flip the can right side up, open it and pour the coconut water out. (Save this for smoothies or as a nutritious addition to soups or sauces.) The firm cream should be the only part left. Scoop into a mixing bowl and follow the recipe as listed above.

Notes: _____

_____

_____

_____

_____

_____

_____

_____

_____

_____

_____

_____

_____

_____

_____

_____

DAY 5: GAME TIME COVERED IN GOODNESS

Suggested Time: 10 minutes

Memory Verse: *Whatever is good and perfect is a gift coming down to us from God our Father, who created all the lights in the heavens. He never changes or casts a shifting shadow.* —James 1:17

Parent Tip: *Present the memory verse to your children and allow them to repeat it several times. Include your own hand gestures and movements to help them remember it more easily.*

Supplies: ☐ 2 Pairs of goggles, ☐ Shaving cream or whipped cream, ☐ 2 Bags of colored miniature marshmallows, ☐ Paper towels and/or baby wipes, ☐ Small, fun (nonfood) prizes or rewards, ☐ Stopwatch, stopwatch app on a smartphone or watch with a second hand, ☐ Upbeat music to play during activity (optional)

Prior to Game:

This game is best played outside or in an area where mess is not an issue, like a kitchen or on an easy-to-clean floor. To ensure easy cleanup, lay towels, trash bags or other items that can be used as dropcloths on the floor.

Game Instructions:

We're going to play a fun game today! Our memory verse today talks about the goodness of God. So, in this game, we'll focus on learning about God's protection, His glory and goodness. But first, let's take a few minutes and discuss what each item in this game represents. *(To reinforce your message, hold items up to show players as you discuss each one.)*

- GOGGLES = **God's protection:** He is our shield and cover, keeping us safe from harm.

- SHAVING CREAM = **God's glory:** God rejoices in our victories. Also, the thankful praise and worship we give to God for His help in our lives.

- MINI MARSHMALLOWS = **God's goodness and blessings:** These are recognized in our character and conduct.

Let's go over the rules of the game so we'll all know how to play. First, we'll make 2 teams. Player 1 will wear the goggles to protect his/her eyes from the shaving cream. Then, player 2 will put shaving cream on his/her partner's chin and cheeks to look like a beard! THEN, when the music begins, player 2 will gently toss marshmallows, aiming for the shaving cream on his/her teammate's face. Let's see who can stick the most marshmallows on his/her partner's beard in 1 minute!

Game Goal:

The player (or team) who sticks the most marshmallows to his/her partner's beard in 1 minute, wins!

Final Word:

This week our memory verse talks about God's protection and glory, His goodness and blessings. Each of these are part of who God is and is reflected in how He interacts with us. He protects us and keeps us safe. He is present in our lives, and He rejoices in our heartfelt praise and worship. He is good to us. He loves to bless His kids. Review what each game item represents and how each characteristic of God can be utilized in your Superkids' everyday lives. Reinforce the concepts of God's protection, glory and goodness as the winning team is presented with fun prizes.

Variation No. 1: Parent Play

Parents, don't miss this opportunity to play with your children. Become one of the participants and make a meaningful memory as well as a powerful lesson.

Variation No. 2: Stopwatch

If you don't have enough players for 2 teams, then give each player a 60-second turn, using a stopwatch, stopwatch app on your smartphone or watch with a second hand. The player who sticks the most marshmallows, wins.

Notes: _____

_____

_____

_____

_____

_____

_____

_____

_____

_____

_____

_____

_____

_____

_____

_____

_____

_____

ACTIVITY PAGE | **GOD'S GLORY REVEALED**

 Memory Verse: Whatever is good and perfect is a gift coming down to us from God our Father, who created all the lights in the heavens. He never changes or casts a shifting shadow. —James 1:17

ANSWER KEY:

Name:_____

This week, you learned of the time Moses was allowed to see God. Now, test your observation skills. Below is a picture of Moses at that historic event, but look closely. There are a few items that don't belong. Find a van, a shop, price tag, a discount label, money, a checklist, a for-sale sign, a chart, a basket and a calculator hidden in the picture.

Notes: _____

_____

_____

_____

_____

_____

_____

_____

_____

_____

_____

_____

_____

_____

_____

_____

_____

_____

_____

_____

_____

_____

_____

_____

_____

_____

_____

_____

_____

_____

_____

_____

_____

_____

_____

_____

_____

WEEK 3: A FRIENDSHIP MADE IN HEAVEN

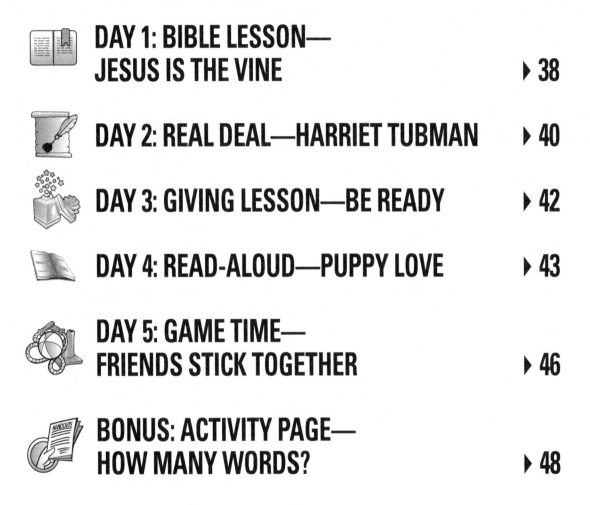

Memory Verse: For the Son of Man came to seek and save those who are lost. —Luke 19:10

WEEK 3: SNAPSHOT — A FRIENDSHIP MADE IN HEAVEN

DAY	TYPE OF LESSON	LESSON TITLE	SUPPLIES
Day 1	Bible Lesson	Jesus Is the Vine	None
Day 2	Real Deal	Harriet Tubman	Pictures of Harriet Tubman
Day 3	Giving Lesson	Be Ready	None
Day 4	Read-Aloud	Puppy Love	Optional Costumes, Props, Art supplies
Day 5	Game Time	Friends Stick Together	Several large balloons, 1 Large feather
Bonus	Activity Page	How Many Words?	1 Copy per child

Lesson Introduction:

One thing children understand is the concept of a best friend. Many of them are discovering what a fun and special experience it is to have someone they are especially close to, someone they can confide in, and most of all, spend every possible moment with! Ask your "super" kids what they like about their best friends, then give examples of how Jesus has shown us what kind of Friend He is.

Discuss the qualities we all desire in a best friend—qualities like loyalty, trustworthiness, honesty, support, generosity and fun. Talk about how Jesus possesses all those qualities, and more. He is the best Friend anyone can ever have, and He wants to be best friends with each of your children.

Love,

Commander Dana

Commander Dana

Lesson Outline:

This week, you will share about Jesus—who He is and the role He desires to have in your children's lives. Take time before you present this lesson to pray about who Jesus is to you and the role He has in your life. Share about what this life-changing relationship means to you and what it can mean to them!

I. JESUS WANTS TO BE YOUR BEST FRIEND

a. God gave His only Son to save us and to win our friendship. John 3:16

b. God wants us to choose life and friendship with Him. Deuteronomy 30:19

c. God made His choice, now it's our turn!

II. JESUS IS A TRUE FRIEND

a. A true friend is always willing to help us. Hebrews 7:25

b. Jesus sacrificed His life for us. John 15:13 says there is no greater love than this!

c. A true friend always stands up for you.

III. REAL FRIENDS GIVE THE HELP YOU NEED

a. Because of sin, we needed our friendship with our Father back.

b. Our Friend Jesus came to defeat death and to bring life to us. John 10:10

c. Jesus gave His life to win our place in heaven! John 15:13

Notes: _____

_____

_____

_____

_____

_____

_____

_____

_____

_____

_____

DAY 1: BIBLE LESSON | JESUS IS THE VINE

 Memory Verse: *For the Son of Man came to seek and save those who are lost.* —Luke 19:10

This is a great opportunity to talk about Jesus' nature and the role He wants to play in your children's lives. He wants to be their best Friend—to help them live successful, loving and overcoming lives. Let this week's Bible lesson be a starting point for you to share what a relationship with Jesus has meant to you. Encourage your children to seek a deep relationship with Jesus for themselves, too!

Read John 15:1-17:
Jesus, the True Vine

I am the true grapevine, and my Father is the gardener. He cuts off every branch of mine that doesn't produce fruit, and he prunes the branches that do bear fruit so they will produce even more. You have already been pruned and purified by the message I have given you. Remain in me, and I will remain in you. For a branch cannot produce fruit if it is severed from the vine, and you cannot be fruitful unless you remain in me.

Yes, I am the vine; you are the branches. Those who remain in me, and I in them, will produce much fruit. For apart from me you can do nothing. Anyone who does not remain in me is thrown away like a useless branch and withers. Such branches are gathered into a pile to be burned. But if you remain in me and my words remain in you, you may ask for anything you want, and it will be granted! When you produce much fruit, you are my true disciples. This brings great glory to my Father.

I have loved you even as the Father has loved me. Remain in my love. When you obey my commandments, you remain in my love, just as I obey my Father's commandments and remain in his love. I have told you these things so that you will be filled with my joy. Yes, your joy will overflow! This is my commandment: Love each other in the same way I have loved you. There is no greater love than to lay down one's life for one's friends. You are my friends if you do what I command. I no longer call you slaves, because a master doesn't confide in his slaves. Now you are my friends, since I have told you everything the Father told me. You didn't choose me. I chose you. I appointed you to go and produce lasting fruit, so that the Father will give you whatever you ask for, using my name. This is my command: Love each other.

Discussion Questions:

1. **Tell me about this passage. What's it about?**

   It's about Jesus, who He is and how He works with the Father.

2. **What did Jesus mean when He said, "I am the true grapevine, and my Father is the gardener"?**

   Jesus gives us life. Just as the branches are connected to the grapevine, we must be connected to Him to receive from Him and enjoy that life. The Father is the "gardener" or caretaker of the vine and master of all.

3. **What did Jesus mean when He said, "Remain in me, and I will remain in you"?**

   Jesus is always with us and lives inside us, and we live in Him, when we ask Him into our hearts to be our Savior. When we stay connected with Him, we become like Him. His nature is reflected in us.

4. **What did Jesus mean when He said, "I am the vine; you are the branches"?**

   As we already learned, Jesus gives us life. His life is reflected in us. We grow and prosper, like branches on a healthy vine, when we remain connected to Him.

5. **What was the final command Jesus gave in this passage?**

   He said to "love each other."

6. **How can we do that?**

   Parents, discuss specific ways your child can love others. Some ideas include:

   - Walking in forgiveness
   - Helping those in need
   - Giving money, time or talent to others
   - Volunteering at church or around the neighborhood
   - Speaking kind words.

Notes: _____

_____

_____

_____

_____

_____

_____

_____

_____

_____

_____

_____

_____

_____

_____

_____

_____

DAY 2: REAL DEAL | **HARRIET TUBMAN**

 Memory Verse: For the Son of Man came to seek and save those who are lost. —Luke 19:10

 Concept: Highlighting an interesting historical place, figure or event that illustrates the theme of the day. The theme of the day is seeking and saving what was lost.

Supplies: ☐ Pictures of Harriet Tubman (from the Internet, a book or perhaps other library resources)

Intro:

Today we've been discussing loyalty and friendship. Can you tell me about our greatest Friend—One who sticks closer to us than any other? *(Allow your children the opportunity to share and discuss the importance of pursuing a friendship with Jesus.)* How does Jesus exhibit friendship to us? *(Through His faithfulness, love, kindness, patience and trustworthiness.)*

For this Real Deal lesson we'll be learning about a woman who demonstrated great loyalty, friendship and perseverance. Her nickname was "Moses," because she led many people out of slavery, just like Moses. Today's Real Deal is about Harriet Tubman. Has anyone heard of her or know anything about her?

Lesson:
About Harriet Tubman:

Historians believe Harriet Tubman was born between 1820 and 1825. No one knows for certain because during this time in American history, there were no formal birth records kept for slaves. Harriet grew up to be a brave, young woman who escaped slavery and went on to lead 13 dangerous rescue missions to free more than 70 friends and family members from slavery.

Harriet's Inspiration—God's Freedom:

Harriet had many terrible experiences as a slave, as did many others, but she chose to believe in and rely on God. She chose to pray for those who hurt her.

When Harriet was a child, her mother read her Bible stories. She learned about God asking Moses to help rescue the children of Israel from slavery. This story continually inspired and motivated Harriet to someday live free and help others experience freedom.

The Great Escape:

Harriet's first attempt to be free lasted only two weeks, but she wouldn't give up! She was determined. She knew it was God's will for people to live free and use their freedom to help others. Her second attempt at freedom was successful, and she began her mission to set others free.

The Underground Railroad:

Harriet's rescue missions were challenging and scary, so she developed what was called an underground railroad system.

The Underground Railroad wasn't really a train. Harriet's system was just called that. It was actually a willing group of people who hid escaped slaves in their homes during the day, kind of like small railroad stations along the "tracks" to freedom. This group of people helped slaves make their journey, just like on a railroad, to freedom without being seen or caught. For most of the slaves Harriet rescued, escaping to freedom was about 90 miles away, which took almost three weeks of travel on foot.

Giving in Secret:

Harriet's rescue missions were top secret, and she helped rescue slaves for 11 years. At the time, she didn't receive any recognition for her bravery, but she continued her missions because she loved God and wanted people to live free.

Outro:

Harriet Tubman said: "I am free, and they should be free." We can choose to live free and help others experience true freedom in Jesus. When we tell others about our Lord and Savior, Jesus, and help them to ask Him into their hearts so they can experience God's love and blessings like we did, we're doing what Harriet Tubman did. We're helping others to be free to love and serve Jesus, too!

Harriet Tubman is an inspiration. Her determination, loyalty, love for God, and commitment to freedom empowered her to rescue many slaves.

Variation: Library Visit

Visit your local library and find an age-appropriate biography about Harriet Tubman to read as a family. Use it as a way to re-emphasize the Christ-like character that Harriet Tubman exhibited.

Notes: _____

_____

_____

_____

_____

_____

_____

_____

_____

_____

DAY 3: GIVING LESSON

BE READY

 Suggested Time: 10 minutes

 Offering Scripture: Does merely talking about faith indicate that a person really has it? For instance, you come upon an old friend dressed in rags and half-starved and say, "Good morning, friend! Be clothed in Christ! Be filled with the Holy Spirit!" and walk off without providing so much as a coat or a cup of soup—where does that get you? —James 2:14-16 MSG

Lesson Instructions:

In today's scripture, James wanted to share about the importance of helping those in need. *(Read the scripture aloud again.)* He says, "Does merely talking about faith indicate that a person really has it? For instance, you come upon an old friend dressed in rags and half-starved and say, 'Good morning, friend! Be clothed in Christ! Be filled with the Holy Spirit!' and walk off without providing so much as a coat or a cup of soup—where does that get you?"

What does this mean to you? *(Allow time for your children to share and discuss what this scripture means to them and how they can live it in their everyday lives.)*

When we meet people who are in need and express real interest in their lives and do something to help, we plant seeds of God's unconditional love and goodness in their hearts. We can choose to be people of love and action by offering help to those in need.

Let's take a moment and write down three ways we can help those in need this week. *(Allow your children an opportunity to share their ideas.)*

Let's look for ways we can put these great ideas into practice! In fact, let's come up with a plan for doing that. *(Take a time to place dates, times and names next to the ideas. Add them to your weekly schedule and place the list in an open place—the refrigerator, the bathroom mirror or family bulletin board. Then, commit to doing the list this week.)*

What an awesome opportunity we have to honor God by giving and helping those in need! Jesus said that when you help people who are in need or sick or can't help themselves, you are really doing it to Him (Matthew 25:31-45)!

Notes: _____

_____

_____

_____

_____

_____

DAY 4: READ-ALOUD | PUPPY LOVE

 Suggested Time: 15 minutes

 Memory Verse: For the Son of Man came to seek and save those who are lost. —Luke 19:10

 Parent Tip: This segment has many possible variations. Choose the one that best fits your family, and have fun!

 List of Characters/Optional Costumes:
- Madison: Elementary school-age girl, winter clothes (coat, scarf and gloves)
- Mom: Dresses, speaks and acts just like your mom, winter clothes (Have fun mimicking your mother.)
- Dad: Dresses, speaks and acts just like your dad (Have fun mimicking your father.)

Supplies: ■ Whiteboard, chalkboard or easel with paper, ■ Markers or pastel chalks, ■ Rags (to blend chalks), ■ Pencil and eraser (art pencils work best), ■ Art smock (to keep your artist's clothes clean)

Variation No. 1:

Read the story as part of your read-aloud time. Reading the story beforehand and giving different voices to each character will help bring life to the story.

Variation No. 2:

Read the story as an old-time radio skit, complete with different actors for each part. If you are limited on participants, then have more than one part per person and change the voice. Make copies of the skit and have each actor highlight their lines.

Variation No. 3:

Act out the story as a fun skit. Perhaps your children can practice during the day (even creating fun costumes from everyday items) and then perform it in the evening before the whole family. Before beginning your skit, remember to introduce your cast!

Variation No. 4:

Create a storybook theater where one or more family members sketch the story on a whiteboard, chalkboard or artist's easel as another member reads the story. Initially, there will be a few supplies to purchase but don't let this be a deterrent from using the illustrated story option! Once the supplies have been purchased, they'll be long-lasting and reusable.

To make your presentation easier, lightly sketch the drawing with a pencil prior to presentation. Time may not allow the picture to be completely drawn and colored at the time of the lesson. Erase pencil lines, so light lines are visible to the artist but not visible to your children. Review the story ahead of time to determine the amount of time needed to complete the illustration while telling the story. When the story begins, use black markers to "draw" the picture, following the sketched pencil lines. Next, apply color using the pastel chalk. Then, blend the color with the rags. Finally, cut the illustration from the board, roll it up, secure it with rubber bands, and share it with one of your children!

Story:

"Mom, when can I have a dog?" Madison asked her mom.

In fact, she asked her mom and dad at least twice a week about getting a dog. Her mother usually gave the same answer, and here it was again: "Pretty soon, Maddie. We just need to find the right dog for our family."

Madison closed her bedroom door and flopped back on her bed. Why did parents say stuff like "pretty soon"? Surely it shouldn't be so hard to find the "right dog" for their family. They just needed to look for it.

Madison had wanted a dog for as long as she could remember. To be more specific, she wanted a puppy that would eventually become a full-grown dog. The thought of having her very own little puppy made her smile.

That night, when Madison climbed into bed, her parents came into her room to pray and tuck her in. Her mom and dad sat on the side of her bed, as her dad said a prayer. "God, watch over Maddie tonight as she sleeps. Keep her close to You all of her life, and give her the desires of her heart. In Jesus' Name. Amen."

Madison looked up at her father. "Daddy, did you really mean that prayer?" she asked.

Her father looked surprised. "Every word!" he replied.

"Because the desire of my heart right now is to have a puppy, and that's what I want more than anything else, but you and Mom always say 'pretty soon' when I ask for one."

"Maybe you should pray and ask God to bring the right dog to us, one that will be the perfect fit for our family," her dad said.

Madison agreed as her parents hugged her and tucked her in. Then, before she went to sleep, Madison decided to talk to God about her dog situation. "Heavenly Father, would You help me find the right puppy for our family, one that will end up being a dog? I really want one, and I will give it all the love it can stand!" With that, Madison turned on her side and fell asleep.

That night, Madison dreamt she had a puppy of her own. He was hiding somewhere in the house, but she could not find him anywhere. "Come here, boy. Come on," Madison coaxed. "Come out, I want to play with you and take care of you!"

The dream seemed to last all night until…

"Maddie, time to wake up. We have to get ready!" Her mom's voice woke her, interrupting her perfectly good dream about puppy hunting.

Madison then remembered they were going to her cousin's house for a visit.

"Let's go! It's a long drive," her mother shouted from the kitchen. "And don't forget to bring your coat, it's getting really cold outside!"

In no time, Madison and her mom were driving to the country. The wind was blowing, and it looked like it could snow.

"I hope we get some snow to play in!" Madison exclaimed.

As they drove along, Madison stared out the window. She was daydreaming about dogs, time with her cousins and playing in the snow.

As they drove past an old road, Madison noticed something. "Mom, I think I saw something along that road!" she said excitedly.

"What was it?" her mother asked.

"I couldn't tell, but it looked like a small animal of some kind. Can we turn around and check?"

Madison's mom looked at her watch, and then at the clouds. "We'll take a quick look, but don't get too close," her mother warned.

As she turned the car around, Madison could feel her heart pounding. She wondered, *What kind of small animal would be out here all alone, in this freezing weather?*

As the car rolled to a stop, Madison got out and walked closer to the road. She bent down and peered at the small animal.

The small animal was huddled in a ball several feet away from her. Madison could see it was shivering. Suddenly, it lifted its head and looked at her. It was a small puppy, half frozen and scared to move. It just sat there, huddled up and shivering.

Madison whispered, "Come here, boy. Come on! We have a warm car for you to ride in." The little puppy didn't move. He seemed to be frozen in place, except for his shivering. Madison didn't know if he was cold or scared or both.

As Madison continued to call him, she suddenly remembered her dream. In her softest voice she whispered, "Come on, little puppy. I just want to play with you and be your best friend."

Suddenly, the puppy took a step. He looked at Madison as she smiled and held her hand out. He took another step, and then another. After what seemed like forever to Madison, the puppy headed toward her outstretched arms.

Just as the snowflakes were beginning to fall, the puppy gave Madison's hand a tiny lick. She carefully picked him up and walked to the car.

"Mom, isn't this amazing?" Her mom was very surprised! "Can I keep him?" Madison asked.

"On one condition," her mother replied. "Only if we cannot find the owner."

"I think someone dumped the puppy out here, Mom," she said. "I'm going to call him Snowflake because I rescued him just before the snowflakes covered the ground." As they rode along, Snowflake snuggled into Maddie's lap. He seemed very content, and even made little noises that made Madison smile.

When Madison went to bed that night, Snowflake slept right beside her in his own warm bed. Before she went to sleep, Madison prayed, "God, thank You SOOOO much for letting me help Snowflake. I promise to love him and take really good care of him."

Sure enough, Snowflake became Madison's puppy. As you can imagine, he grew up having the best life a puppy could ask for. And eventually, Snowflake became a full-grown dog.

DAY 5: GAME TIME | **FRIENDS STICK TOGETHER**

 Suggested Time: 10-12 minutes

Memory Verse: For the Son of Man came to seek and save those who are lost. —Luke 19:10

 Parent Tip: Present the memory verse to your children and allow them to repeat it several times. Include your own hand gestures and movements to help them remember it more easily.

 Supplies: ■ Several large balloons, ■ 1 Large feather

Prior to Lesson:

Inflate the balloons to near capacity. Place the feather on a table or chair in front of your children.

Game Instructions:

Has anyone heard the saying, "Birds of a feather stick together"? And does anyone know what this saying means? *(Allow your children to share and discuss their ideas.)*

Those are some interesting thoughts!

We can think of it like this: When friends are devoted to each other, they stick together. It's important to ask God to help you choose good friends. If your friend shares a great experience with you, it's important to be excited and happy with them. If your friend experiences a challenging or sad situation, it's important to support and encourage him/her.

In our game today, we'll practice what it means to be birds of a feather who stick together, and we'll discover who can stick together the best! *(Allow your children to choose a partner, or count off 1-2, 1-2, etc.)*

OK, let's have our players stand back-to-back and gently support a balloon between them. I'm going to put this feather on the stand behind the finish line. Each 2 players with the balloon gently pushed together between their backs, must walk that way, all the way to the finish line, pick up the feather and shout, "We stick together!" without dropping the balloon. Team members can't use their arms or hands to steady the balloon. If a team happens to drop the balloon, players must return to the starting line and start again!

Game Goal:

The first team to reach the finish line, grab the feather and shout, "We stick together!" wins.

Final Word:

What did it take to play this game? And, how did it feel to work together? *(Allow discussion.)*

Being a loyal friend means choosing to stick together by supporting and encouraging each other. It also means we choose to care for the needs of others, not just for ourselves. God wants us to be loyal friends and stick together!

Variation: Parent Play

Parents, don't miss this opportunity to play with your children. Become a participant, and make a meaningful memory as well as a powerful lesson. Consider playing parents against kids or even switching out teammates to see which combination of players gets the best time.

Notes: _____

_____

_____

_____

_____

_____

_____

_____

_____

_____

_____

_____

_____

_____

_____

_____

_____

_____

_____

_____

_____

_____

ACTIVITY PAGE **HOW MANY WORDS?**

Memory Verse: For the Son of Man came to seek and save those who are lost. —Luke 19:10

ANSWER KEY:

FRIENDSHIP

ANSWER KEY:

YOU CAN SPELL MORE THAN 300 WORDS USING THE LETTERS FOUND IN FRIENDSHIP. HERE IS A SAMPLING:

DENS	HEIRS	RINSED
DIES	HIDES	RIPENS
DINES	HIRES	RISEN
DINERS	INSIDER	SEND
DISH	INSPIRED	SHINE
ENDS	IRISH	SHRED
FENDS	PENS	SHRINE
FERNS	PINES	SNIDE
FRESH	PRIDE	SNIPER
FRIED	REFINISH	SPED
FRIENDS	RESIN	SPEND
FRIES	RIDES	SPIDER

Name:_____

This week, you've learned that Jesus wants to be your best Friend. Find out how many words (three letters or more) you can make out of the letters in the word FRIENDSHIP. Try to find at least 30.

FRIENDSHIP

1. _____	11. _____	21. _____
2. _____	12. _____	22. _____
3. _____	13. _____	23. _____
4. _____	14. _____	24. _____
5. _____	15. _____	25. _____
6. _____	16. _____	26. _____
7. _____	17. _____	27. _____
8. _____	18. _____	28. _____
9. _____	19. _____	29. _____
10. _____	20. _____	30. _____

Notes: _____

_____

_____

_____

_____

_____

_____

_____

_____

_____

_____

_____

_____

_____

_____

_____

_____

_____

_____

_____

_____

_____

_____

_____

_____

_____

_____

_____

_____

_____

_____

_____

_____

_____

_____

_____

_____

_____

WEEK 4: THE HOLY SPIRIT, OUR HELPER

Memory Verse: When the Friend comes, the Spirit of the Truth, he will take you by the hand and guide you into all the truth there is. —John 16:13 MSG

WEEK 4 SNAPSHOT

THE HOLY SPIRIT, OUR HELPER

DAY	TYPE OF LESSON	LESSON TITLE	SUPPLIES
Day 1	Bible Lesson	The Promise of the Holy Spirit	None
Day 2	Object Lesson	The Best Tour Guide	Favorite foreign-country tour-guide book or U.S. vacation-destination information booklet (optional), Pictures from a favorite vacation (optional), Pen/paper, computer or tablet
Day 3	Giving Lesson	God Time	Small gift items
Day 4	Food Fun	Things That Go Together	Small plates and/or bowls (if choosing to share food items with kids), Cookies, 2 Small glasses of milk, Cheese slices, Crackers, Vanilla ice cream, Chocolate syrup
Day 5	Game Time	Follow Your Guide	8-10 Large rubber cones, 4 Hula hoops, Hula hoop stands or have kids support hoops, 2 Blindfolds, Stopwatch, stopwatch app on your smartphone or watch with a second hand
Bonus	Activity Page	Apostles' Maze	1 Copy for each child

Lesson Introduction:

The Holy Spirit was sent from heaven to be our Friend and Helper. That is so important because it means God is always right here with us. He is here, He is available and He is working. We can ask the Holy Spirit to help us be good friends and to care about the needs of others, and He will use us to do just that.

Thanking the Father daily for the gifts He has given us is one way to honor Him and grow in our frienship with Him. Let's take a few minutes and thank God for sending us the ultimate Helper, the Holy Spirit!

Love,

Commander Dana

Commander Dana

Lesson Outline:

So often, the Body of Christ overlooks or dismisses the work of the Holy Spirit. That's why this week is such a special time. You will introduce your children to the Holy Spirit and the work He does in our lives. He did not pass away. He did not leave. He is here with us. Savor this time. Let it be the beginning of a deeper understanding for them—and you—as you introduce them to the third member of the Godhead.

I. THE HOLY SPIRIT IS OUR COUNSELOR AND GUIDE John 14:26

a.   The Holy Spirit is a gift from the Father.

b.   The Holy Spirit continues the work of Jesus in the world. John 15:26

c.   The Holy Spirit will help us make godly, God-led decisions!

II. THE HOLY SPIRIT WILL TEACH US

a.   The Holy Spirit is our "Truth Guide." John 16:13

b.   The Holy Spirit will teach us about things to come. John 16:13

c.   Being filled with the Holy Spirit is like having your own "personal trainer"!

III. THE HOLY SPIRIT LIVES IN US

a.   We ask God for the Holy Spirit in our lives. Luke 11:13

b.   When you receive the Holy Spirit, you receive power! Acts 1:8

c.   When the Holy Spirit lives in us, we become a "powerhouse"!

Notes: _____

_____

_____

_____

_____

_____

_____

_____

_____

_____

DAY 1: BIBLE LESSON | **THE PROMISE OF THE HOLY SPIRIT**

Memory Verse: When the Friend comes, the Spirit of the Truth, he will take you by the hand and guide you into all the truth there is. —John 16:13 MSG

This week's Bible lesson recounts Jesus' promise of the Holy Spirit's arrival just before His ascension, or going back into heaven. This was an important moment in history. Not only did the apostles see Jesus leave, but He promised that the Holy Spirit would bring power, making it possible for them to do all God the Father had called them to do. And thankfully, the Holy Spirit's still making that possible today!

Read Acts 1:1-11:
The Promise of the Holy Spirit

In my first book I told you, Theophilus, about everything Jesus began to do and teach until the day he was taken up to heaven after giving his chosen apostles further instructions through the Holy Spirit. During the forty days after he suffered and died, he appeared to the apostles from time to time, and he proved to them in many ways that he was actually alive. And he talked to them about the Kingdom of God.

Once when he was eating with them, he commanded them, "Do not leave Jerusalem until the Father sends you the gift he promised, as I told you before. John baptized with water, but in just a few days you will be baptized with the Holy Spirit."

The Ascension of Jesus

So when the apostles were with Jesus, they kept asking him, "Lord, has the time come for you to free Israel and restore our kingdom?"

He replied, "The Father alone has the authority to set those dates and times, and they are not for you to know. But you will receive power when the Holy Spirit comes upon you. And you will be my witnesses, telling people about me everywhere—in Jerusalem, throughout Judea, in Samaria, and to the ends of the earth."

After saying this, he was taken up into a cloud while they were watching, and they could no longer see him. As they strained to see him rising into heaven, two white-robed men suddenly stood among them. "Men of Galilee," they said, "why are you standing here staring into heaven? Jesus has been taken from you into heaven, but someday he will return from heaven in the same way you saw him go!"

Discussion Questions:

1. **Tell me what happens in this passage.**

   During the 40 days between Jesus rising from the dead and going up into heaven, He met with His followers to teach them. Right before He went up into heaven, Jesus promised the apostles that the Holy Spirit was coming and that they should not leave Jerusalem until He did.

2. **What did Jesus mean when He said John baptized with water but they would be baptized with the Holy Spirit?**

John the Baptist baptized people with water, just as he baptized Jesus, but there is a different kind of baptism—the Baptism in the Holy Spirit. That's when believers are filled with the Spirit of God, with the evidence of praying in other tongues. Jesus wanted His disciples to receive this empowerment.

3. **What would this new Baptism in the Holy Spirit allow them to do?**

The Baptism in the Holy Spirit would help the apostles to do God's work with the same power He has.

4. **What kind of work did Jesus tell the apostles the Holy Spirit would allow them to do?**

They would be able to be Jesus' witnesses and tell others about Him.

5. **What kind of work do you believe the Holy Spirit has called us to do?**

Parents, discuss this with your children. They are able to share Jesus with their friends in the neighborhood, at school and even in church. Brainstorm specifics of how they can do this. They can share the gospel outright, invite friends to church, befriend someone who is lonely, care for those in need, volunteer at church and more. By making this specific, it makes it even more real for them. Follow up later in the week to encourage your children to be persistent and follow through.

Notes: _____

_____

_____

_____

_____

_____

_____

_____

_____

_____

_____

_____

_____

_____

_____

_____

_____

_____

_____

DAY 2: OBJECT LESSON | **THE BEST TOUR GUIDE**

 Suggested Time: 5-7 minutes

 Memory Verse: When the Friend comes, the Spirit of the Truth, he will take you by the hand and guide you into all the truth there is. —John 16:13 MSG

Supplies: ■ Favorite foreign-country tour-guide book or U.S. vacation-destination information booklet (optional), ■ Pictures from a favorite vacation (optional), ■ Pen/paper, computer or tablet

Lesson Instructions:

Hey, Superkids! Today, we're going to discuss our favorite vacation destinations.

Who likes to take vacations and travel?

Can anyone tell me about one of the favorite places you've traveled to? (*Allow time for the children to share their experiences.*)

It's always an adventure to travel to new places, and it's also an adventure to enjoy the area and the people who live there.

So, here's another question: If you could go anywhere in the world, where would it be? (*Allow time for your children to share their dreams. Now, take time to share your favorite travel experiences or favorite vacation spot. It would be great to share pictures, guide books, souvenirs, etc. Help your children experience as much as possible from your favorite travel experience. It will be fun taking them on "vacation" with you!*)

You know what would be really fun! Let's make a faith list of the places you'd like to visit. (*Record the list of places using pen/paper, computer or tablet.*) Let's pray over our list and believe God together to be able to go on these trips!

Traveling can be challenging but lots of fun! Our memory verse today is John 16:13 (MSG): "When the Friend comes, the Spirit of the Truth, he will take you by the hand and guide you into all the truth there is."

We're talking about traveling to real places on real adventures, but did you know that the Holy Spirit can take us on adventures close to home, too? He can lead us in whatever He has planned for us.

He can do this for physical travel plans, and He can do it for spiritual travel plans. He's our guide through everything we do throughout our lives. He will lead us in the right direction every time!

Notes: _____

_____

_____

_____

DAY 3: GIVING LESSON

GOD TIME

Suggested Time: 10 minutes

Offering Scripture: Now we have not received the spirit [that belongs to] the world, but the [Holy] Spirit Who is from God, [given to us] so that we might realize and comprehend and appreciate the gifts [of divine favor and blessing so freely and lavishly] bestowed on us by God. —1 Corinthians 2:12 AMPC

Supplies: ☐ Small gift items (like from the dollar store)

Lesson Instructions:

Do you like Christmas? What is the best thing about Christmas? *(Allow your children to share their favorite parts of Christmas.)*

It's always great to receive gifts at Christmas, but the best gifts are the ones we give others. Our lives will be so much more enjoyable when we look for ways to bless other people. God, our Father, is the ultimate gift giver! He blesses our lives each day with protection, love, favor, peace, joy and more.

Just like our offering scripture today from 1 Corinthians 2:12, we can ask the Holy Spirit to help us recognize the gifts that God has given us in our lives each day.

We also want to take time to thank our heavenly Father for His goodness in our lives. We can call these moments, "God time"!

"God time" is when we stop what we're doing, and thank God for doing something special in our lives.

I have a few small gifts I would like to share with you today! *(While passing out the small gifts, encourage kids to share and express thankfulness to the Father for His goodness in their lives each day.)*

Let's take a few moments of "God time" and thank God for all the gifts He gives us. Now, let's honor Him by preparing our offering for this week's church service.

Notes: _____

_____

_____

_____

_____

_____

_____

_____

_____

DAY 4: FOOD FUN | **THINGS THAT GO TOGETHER**

 Suggested Time: 10 minutes

 Memory Verse: When the Friend comes, the Spirit of the Truth, he will take you by the hand and guide you into all the truth there is. —John 16:13 MSG

Supplies: ■ Small plates and/or bowls (if choosing to share food items with kids), ■ Cookies, ■ 2 Small glasses of milk, ■ Cheese slices, ■ Crackers, ■ Vanilla ice cream, ■ Chocolate syrup

Prior to Lesson:

Place the food items in random order on the table.

Lesson Instructions:

In our lesson today, we'll be sharing different foods that taste great together. Each of you can take some foods that go together to make a great team—like milk and cookies, cheese and crackers, ice cream and chocolate. Mmmmm! They all sound yummy! *(Invite children to sample the food items on the table.)*

Can we think of anything else that would make a great team? *(Allow kids to offer ideas and discuss.)*

I think I have a winning combination! What about being a great friend and having great friends? Friends make wonderful teams!

We can also thank God for sending us the Holy Spirit to be our Counselor and Friend. No matter who we are, He's always a great Partner—a great team member—and we are always better when we're connected to Him!

Notes: _____

_____

_____

_____

_____

_____

_____

_____

_____

_____

_____

DAY 5: GAME TIME   FOLLOW YOUR GUIDE

Suggested Time: 5-10 Minutes

Memory Verse: When the Friend comes, the Spirit of the Truth, he will take you by the hand and guide you into all the truth there is. —John 16:13 MSG

Teacher Tip: Present the memory verse to your children and allow them to repeat it several times. Include your own hand gestures and movements to help them remember it more easily.

Supplies: ■ 8-10 Large rubber cones, ■ 4 Hula hoops, ■ Hula hoop stands or have kids support hoops, ■ 2 Blindfolds, ■ Stopwatch, stopwatch app on your smartphone or watch with a second hand

Prior to Game:

Create an obstacle course. Make a line of cones and hold a hula hoop vertically. Assign one participant as the "guide" (representing the Holy Spirit) and the other as the follower.

Game Instructions:

In our fun game, today, we'll be navigating through an obstacle course! I know all of you can do this easily. But, there's a catch! You have to be a really good listener and directions-follower to win!

So, who has *really* good ears to hear? *(Choose a Superkid to demonstrate how the game is played.)*

So, what's the catch? I know all of you can do this obstacle course easily, but how about blindfolded? Not as easy, is it?

Let's do a little demonstration. First, we'll blindfold the player. *(Apply blindfold to the helper.)* OK, now comes the tricky part! You'll have to really listen because the guide will only help you with words. *(Allow the guide to lead the follower through a little of the course, using only words.)*

We're going to time each player, so the better you listen and do what the guide says, the faster you'll finish! The player with the fastest time will win.

The guide will navigate you through the obstacle course as you weave through or around the cones and climb through the hula hoop by listening to his/her instructions. When the blindfolded player finishes the course, the guide will switch places with the follower and start at the beginning of the obstacle course.

Game Goal:

The player with the fastest time, wins!

Final Word:

In our game, the guides led the followers through the obstacle course as smoothly and accurately as possible. Our memory verse tells us that the Holy Spirit will take us by the hand and guide us into all truth. We can resist Him, or choose to listen and be good followers. When we learn to listen and follow Him well, He will always guide us into The Sweet Life of His blessings!

The Holy Spirit is a wonderful gift and a great blessing to our lives. He is our Helper and Guide. We can ask Him to help guide us throughout every day.

Variation No. 1: Parent Play

Parents, don't miss this opportunity to play with your children. Become one of the participants and make a meaningful memory as well as a powerful lesson.

Variation No. 2: Common Items

If you don't own cones and hula hoops, create an obstacle course using items from your house. Chairs, cardboard boxes, sports equipment, etc., can all be used to create obstacles around which participants can navigate.

Notes: _____

_____

_____

_____

_____

_____

_____

_____

_____

_____

_____

_____

_____

_____

_____

_____

_____

_____

ACTIVITY PAGE

APOSTLES' MAZE

Memory Verse: When the Friend comes, the Spirit of the Truth, he will take you by the hand and guide you into all the truth there is. —John 16:13 MSG

ANSWER KEY:

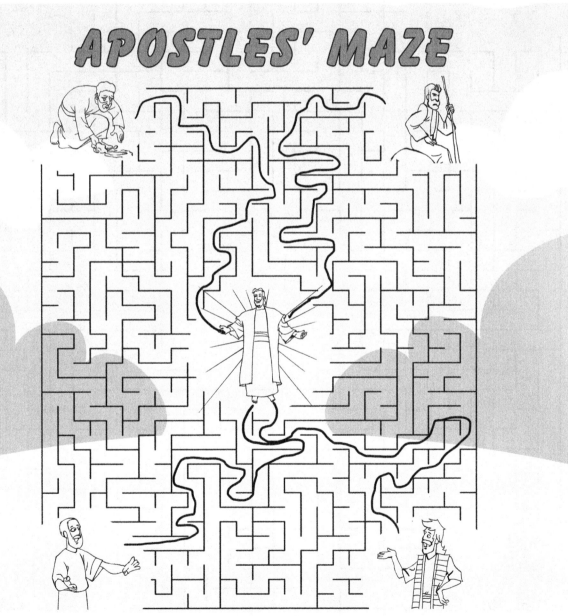

Name:_____

In our Bible lesson this week, Jesus told the apostles not to leave Jerusalem until God sent the Holy Spirit. After His Resurrection, He spent several days teaching them. In this maze, help the apostles come from all over Jerusalem to learn from Jesus.

APOSTLES' MAZE

WEEK 5: YOUR SECRET LANGUAGE

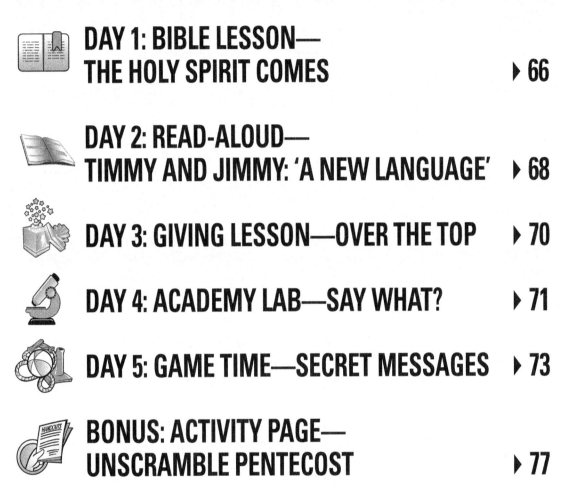

Memory Verse: And these signs will follow those who believe: In My name they will cast out demons; they will speak with new tongues. —Mark 16:17 NKJV

63

WEEK 5: SNAPSHOT   YOUR SECRET LANGUAGE

DAY	TYPE OF LESSON	LESSON TITLE	SUPPLIES
Day 1	Bible Lesson	The Holy Spirit Comes	None
Day 2	Read-Aloud	Timmy and Jimmy: 'A New Language'	None
Day 3	Giving Lesson	Over the Top	2 Scoops of vanilla ice cream, 1 Can of root beer, 1 Ice-cream scoop, 1 Large, clear glass
Day 4	Academy Lab	Say What?	Water, Baking soda, Q-tips®, White paper, Lamp, Purple grape juice, Small paintbrush
Day 5	Game Time	Secret Messages	1 Large sheet of poster paper and marker or chalkboard/chalk, Big dice, Prizes
Bonus	Activity Page	Unscramble Pentecost	1 Copy for each child

Lesson Introduction:

This week, you have a great opportunity to share about the power God's Word tells us is available when we receive the Holy Spirit. It is the ability to speak in a new prayer language—in other tongues. This is important because Jesus sent the Holy Spirit to help us and comfort us. When we're not quite sure what to pray, we can use our prayer language (Romans 8:26-27).

If your children have yet to receive their prayer language, you have a great opportunity to lead them in that experience. Acts 19:6 gives you the model for leading them in that prayer. Pray with them, lay hands on them and then pray in the spirit together.

Love,

Commander Dana

Commander Dana

Lesson Outline:

Leading your children in the profound and life-changing experience of receiving the Baptism in the Holy Spirit is priceless. Spend some time in prayer about this lesson. Ask the Holy Spirit to lead you as you lead them in prayer about it. He is faithful!

I. OUR FATHER PROMISED US AN AWESOME GIFT Acts 1:4

a.   Jesus said receiving the Holy Spirit was a baptism. Verse 5

b.   Water baptism gets you completely, 100 percent, wet.

c.   Baptism in the Holy Spirit gets you completely filled!

II. THE HOLY SPIRIT CAME TO US NOISILY AND VISIBLY Acts 2:1-3

a.   The Holy Spirit did not sneak to earth quietly.

b.   He sounded like a loud windstorm and looked like fire.

c.   Great things happen when God's children come together in unity!

III. A HEAVENLY LANGUAGE IS AVAILABLE TO EVERYONE

a.   God's Word calls this "speaking in other tongues." Acts 2:4 (KJV)

b.   In our prayer language, our spirits pray directly to God. 1 Corinthians 14:2

c.   The Holy Spirit and powerful witnessing go together. Acts 2:8

Notes: _____

_____

_____

_____

_____

_____

_____

_____

_____

_____

_____

DAY 1: BIBLE LESSON THE HOLY SPIRIT COMES

Memory Verse: *And these signs will follow those who believe: In My name they will cast out demons; they will speak with new tongues.* —Mark 16:17 NKJV

This week's Bible lesson shares about the Holy Spirit's arrival. What a historic time that was! It was the fulfillment of a promise and the giving of a Comforter. No longer was the Spirit of God to be kept in the Ark of the Covenant or the Tabernacle. Now, the Holy Spirit would indwell God's people…and He still indwells His people today. Enjoy sharing this powerful history and truth with your children!

Read Acts 2:1-11:
The Holy Spirit Comes

On the day of Pentecost all the believers were meeting together in one place. Suddenly, there was a sound from heaven like the roaring of a mighty windstorm, and it filled the house where they were sitting. Then, what looked like flames or tongues of fire appeared and settled on each of them. And everyone present was filled with the Holy Spirit and began speaking in other languages, as the Holy Spirit gave them this ability.

At that time there were devout Jews from every nation living in Jerusalem. When they heard the loud noise, everyone came running, and they were bewildered to hear their own languages being spoken by the believers.

They were completely amazed. "How can this be?" they exclaimed. "These people are all from Galilee, and yet we hear them speaking in our own native languages! Here we are—Parthians, Medes, Elamites, people from Mesopotamia, Judea, Cappadocia, Pontus, the province of Asia, Phrygia, Pamphylia, Egypt, and the areas of Libya around Cyrene, visitors from Rome (both Jews and converts to Judaism), Cretans, and Arabs. And we all hear these people speaking in our own languages about the wonderful things God has done!"

Discussion Questions:

1. **Describe three things that happened in this passage.**

   Answers will vary, but ensure that your children understand the passage.

2. **Do you think the disciples who were from Galilee understood what they were saying when the Holy Spirit came upon them and they began speaking in tongues?**

   No, they didn't, but they were being obedient and allowing the Holy Spirit to flow through them as they yielded to Him.

3. **How did their obedience to pray in other tongues affect those around them?**

   The listeners were able to hear the wonderful things God had done, in their own languages.

4. **What can we learn from this passage about speaking in tongues?**

The Holy Spirit speaks through us when we yield our tongues to Him as we pray in the spirit. Whether we're praying in a group or on our own, we're allowing Him to flow through us.

5. **Parents/teachers, share about your own experience of praying in the spirit. Why do you do it? How do you do it? When do you do it? What results have you achieved?**

6. **Ask your children if they would like you to pray with them to receive the Holy Spirit. If they are willing, lay hands on them and pray for the Holy Spirit to give them their prayer language. Then, pray in the spirit together.**

Notes: _____

_____

_____

_____

_____

_____

_____

_____

_____

_____

_____

_____

_____

_____

_____

_____

_____

_____

_____

_____

_____

_____

_____

_____

_____

DAY 2: READ-ALOUD

| TIMMY & JIMMY: 'A NEW LANGUAGE' |

 Suggested Time: 15 minutes

 Memory Verse: And these signs will follow those who believe: In My name they will cast out demons; they will speak with new tongues. —Mark 16:17 NKJV

Background:

This week, your children will hear a story about two best friends and their conversation about receiving the Baptism in the Holy Spirit and their prayer language. Use this opportunity to minister to your children the importance of receiving the Baptism in the Holy Spirit and their prayer language!

Story:

It was Wednesday night and Timmy and Jimmy, two best friends, were meeting to go to their youth group. Timmy had agreed to meet at Jimmy's house since he was always so punctual. In fact, Timmy was generally early; whereas Jimmy, a carefree spirit, believed being 10 minutes late was the equivalent of being right on time.

Timmy rang the doorbell and waited. Jimmy opened it, his face morphing into different contorted shapes. "Come on in. Just doing my 'speaking in tongues' warmups."

Timmy, always in awe of the twists and turns of his friend's mind, asked cautiously, "You warm up to speak in tongues?"

"Yeah," Jimmy stated seriously. "Well, I'm still learning, anyway." He continued to contort his face.

Motioning his thumb back toward the door, Timmy asked, "Do you want me to leave?"

"No, you can stay. As long as you don't care if I practice," he said, with more contortions.

Timmy raised his hands in surrender. "Go right ahead."

"Tequita tu taco. Tequita tu taco. Tequita tu taco," Jimmy began reciting over and over again.

Timmy watched in wonder. "That sounds like Spanish."

"It *is* Spanish."

"I thought you were going to speak in tongues," Timmy asked.

"I did."

Timmy squinted skeptically. "No, that was Spanish."

"Same thing." Jimmy shrugged.

"No, it's really not," Timmy said slowly. "Speaking in tongues is speaking in a new language—one you don't know."

"I know. Spanish *is* a new language," Jimmy reasoned. "I've never spoken it before."

Timmy shook his head again. "Sometimes, I don't understand how we're best friends."

"Because we've known each other since we were two, and had matching Spiderman pajamas."

Timmy pressed on, "As I was saying, speaking in tongues is not just learning to speak Spanish."

"Is it Russian? *Das vee don ya!*"

"No! It's…"

"Chinese?" Jimmy interrupted. *"Nee-how!"*

"Jimmy!" Timmy erupted, trying to get his friend back on track. "Tongues is not learning to speak any of those languages—it's a secret language, a prayer language that is between you and God."

Jimmy stopped his contorting and looked at his friend. "That's awesome! So how do I learn it? I hope it's not hard. I've been studying Spanish all week, and my brain's a little foggy."

"That's one of the coolest things about your prayer language. You don't have to learn it," Timmy explained. "The Holy Spirit's language is a special gift from God to us. All we have to do is believe and ask God for it."

"That's so much easier than learning Spanish!" Jimmy agreed. "Just believe and ask? Then what?"

"The Holy Spirit gives you the words to speak," Timmy said. "You don't even have to make them up."

"Wow, so I don't need to warm up before youth group or anything?" Jimmy asked incredulously.

"No, you just need to ask for it."

"Well, let's get to asking," Jimmy said. "We've got a youth group meeting to get to!"

The two friends gave each other a high-five and then bent their heads to pray.

Discussion Questions:

1. **What happened in this story?**

   Answers will vary, but make sure your children understand the story.

2. **What did Jimmy think he had to do to receive his prayer language?**

   He thought he had to practice and learn to speak a foreign language.

3. **What did Timmy teach him about receiving his prayer language?**

   Timmy told Jimmy he just needed to ask God for it. He didn't need to practice or learn a foreign language. He learned that his prayer language is a free gift from the Lord.

Notes: _____

_____

_____

DAY 3: GIVING LESSON OVER THE TOP

 Suggested Time: 10 minutes

 Offering Scripture: I'm singing at the top of my lungs, I'm so full of answered prayers.
—Psalm 13:6 MSG

Supplies: ☐ 2 Scoops of vanilla ice cream, ☐ 1 Can of root beer, ☐ 1 Ice-cream scoop, ☐ 1 Large, clear glass

Lesson Instructions:

For our offering lesson demonstration, I have a few yummy supplies. I have a large glass, some ice cream and a can of root beer.

Can you guess what we'll be making?

Yes, a root beer float! Now, before we combine all the ingredients, let's read our offering scripture together from Psalm 13:6. *(Read the scripture aloud. Add the ingredients as they are discussed in reference to this scripture.)*

Let's imagine this glass is like our lives. The ice cream is similar to answered prayers, and the root beer *(adding enough for it to overflow)* is like us singing at the top of our lungs in worship to God!

When we realize how good God is to us, we can't help but be thankful. We express that thankfulness through praise and worship. Just like this root beer, we'll overflow with His praises!

The same thing is true of our giving. We'll give extravagantly when we realize just how extravagantly the Lord has given to us. Whether it is our money, our time, our talents or our possessions, just like Him, we can be extravagant, overflowing givers.

Who would like to sample our yummy root beer float? *(Share the treat with your children, and allow them to finish.)*

Now, let's prepare our extravagant, overflowing offering for this week's service!

Notes: _____

_____

_____

_____

_____

_____

_____

_____

DAY 4: ACADEMY LAB

SAY WHAT?

Suggested Time: 10 minutes

Memory Verse: *And these signs will follow those who believe: In My name they will cast out demons; they will speak with new tongues.* —Mark 16:17 NKJV

Supplies: ☐ Water, ☐ Baking soda, ☐ Q-Tips®, ☐ White paper, ☐ Lamp, ☐ Purple grape juice, ☐ Small paintbrush

Prior to Lesson:

For optimum results, practice the activity beforehand. It'll help you work through any challenges and give you the ability to present the material seamlessly.

Lesson Instructions:

Do you have a special way of saying or doing things with a best friend that only the two of you can understand? Well, today, we have the opportunity to write our own secret messages to each other. We'll create our own invisible ink!

First, we'll mix together equal parts water and baking soda *(a couple of tablespoons of each)*. Then, we'll pull a little cotton off the tip of the Q-tip to create a firmer writing tip. *(Consider dampening the cotton to make it easier to "write" with.)*

Now, we'll dip the Q-tip in the baking-soda solution and "write" a secret message on the white paper. I have a secret message I'm thinking of that I'm going to try out. *(Write: "God has a secret prayer language for you," and allow it to dry as the lesson continues. Turn the lamp on so it has time to get hot while you're teaching the lesson. Also write the same message on another piece of paper so you can demonstrate the grape-juice reveal with that sample.)*

Are you just a little curious about what I wrote on the paper? It's fun to decode secret messages, isn't it?

Before we find out what's written for our secret message, let's talk a little about a special prayer language that is only between each of us and God. In our memory verse today, we learned that God has a special prayer language available to us, and when we choose to pray in the spirit, we're sharing our hearts with God. When we pray in the spirit, only God knows what we're praying. It's like a special prayer message sent directly to God.

Speaking of special secret messages, now would be a good time to reveal the secret message written on this paper! If we hold the dry paper up to this light bulb, which has gotten really hot, the heat from the bulb will cause the writing on the paper to turn brown, and the message will be revealed! *(Hold the paper up to the lightbulb so the heat can brown the writing.)*

Did you know there's another way to reveal the secret message? If we don't want to use the heat method, we can paint over the secret message with purple grape juice. Purple grape juice? Yup. The chemical reaction between the baking soda and the grape juice will cause the message to turn a different color so the message will be revealed. *(Paint your second sample with the purple grape juice, and hold it up so the kids can see the message.)*

Yes, Superkids, God has a secret prayer language just for you. Having a special prayer language that's only shared between you and God is an *awesome* gift!

Notes: _____

_____

_____

_____

_____

_____

_____

_____

_____

_____

_____

_____

_____

_____

_____

_____

_____

_____

_____

_____

_____

_____

_____

_____

_____

_____

DAY 5: GAME TIME | **SECRET MESSAGES**

 Suggested Time: *8-10 minutes*

 Memory Verse: *And these signs will follow those who believe: In My name they will cast out demons; they will speak with new tongues.* —Mark 16:17 NKJV

 Teacher Tip: *Present the memory verse to your children and allow them to repeat it several times. Include your own hand gestures and movements to help them remember it more easily.*

Supplies: ■ 1 Large sheet of poster paper and marker (or chalkboard and chalk), ■ Secret Message Key, ■ Big dice, ■ Prizes

Prior to Game:

This game is played similarly to "Wheel of Fortune," so each space on the game board represents one letter in the phrase.

Two phrases are provided in this book and can be printed or typed in advance. Prepare the game board and key using a large poster paper and a marker, or chalkboard and chalk. As the judge/host, you will hold the Secret Message Key, which tells you what the secret message is. Throughout the game, play up the fact that you have the key, so you know the secret message. This is important for the point of the game.

Game Instructions:

We have an exciting game today! But, it's going to involve some detective work! Who's ready to be a detective today? We'll split into 2 teams, and each team will work together to decode a "secret message."

Each team will roll the dice to determine which one goes first. The team with the highest roll will start the game.

The starting team will choose a letter. If the letter appears in the secret message, I'll write it in its place. Then, that team will choose again. If the letter doesn't appear in the phrase, then the other team will have a chance to choose a letter.

We'll continue playing until one team (during its turn), decides it can solve the secret message. The first team to solve the message, wins 1 point!

There's a chance to win a bonus point by answering what the secret message is referring to. In other words, the secret message is a hint for the bonus answer. So for each round, you have the chance to win 2 points.

We have 2 messages, so there's a chance for both teams to win a round.

Game Goal:

The first team to solve the "secret message," wins! *(Game boards are located on the next page.)*

Final Word:

Praying in the spirit, or speaking in tongues, is similar to a secret message. What we speak in our prayer language is a mystery to everyone but God. He's the only One with the key!

Variation No. 1: Parent Play

Parents, don't miss this opportunity to play with your children. Become one of the participants and make a meaningful memory as well as a powerful lesson.

Variation No. 2: "Hangman"

If you have only 1 player, play this like "hangman" with your child.

Notes: _____

_____

_____

_____

_____

_____

_____

_____

_____

_____

_____

_____

_____

_____

_____

_____

_____

_____

_____

_____

_____

GAME BOARD #1:

___ ___ ___   ___ ___ ___ ___
1   2   3   4   5   6   7

___ ___ ___ ___ ___
8   9   10   11   12

___ ___ ___ ___ ___ ___ ___ ___   ___ ___
13   14   15   16   17   18   19   20   21   22

SECRET MESSAGE KEY

A-0	B-0	C-0	D-1	E-3	F-1	G-1	H-1
			20	3, 9 19	6	4	2

I-2	J-1	K-0	L-0	M-1	N-0	O-1	P-1
5, 17	8			16		15	13

Q-0	R-1	S-4	T-2	U-2	V-0	W-0	X-0
	14	10, 12 18, 22	1, 7	11, 21			

Y-0	Z-0

Secret Message:
THE GIFT JESUS PROMISED US

Bonus Answer:
THE HOLY SPIRIT

GAME BOARD #2:

___ ___ ___   ___ ___ ___   ___ ___ ___
 1   2   3   4   5   6   7   8   9

___ ___ ___ ___   ___ ___ ___ ___ ___ ___
 10   11   12   13   14   15   16   17   18   19

___ ___ ___ ___
 20   21   22   23

SECRET MESSAGE KEY

A-2	B-0	C-1	D-1	E-3	F-0	G-0	H-3
5, 21		20	4	3, 9 23			2, 8 10

I-2	J-0	K-0	L-1	M-1	N-0	O-1	P-1
16, 18			12	22		11	15

Q-0	R-1	S-1	T-3	U-0	V-0	W-0	X-0
	17	14	1, 7 19				

Y-2	Z-0
6, 13	

Secret Message:
THE DAY THE HOLY SPIRIT CAME

Bonus Answer:
PENTECOST

ACTIVITY PAGE — UNSCRAMBLE PENTECOST

Suggested Time: 10-12 minutes

Memory Verse: And these signs will follow those who believe: In My name, they will cast out demons; they will speak with new tongues. —Mark 16:17 NKJV

ANSWER KEY:

UNSCRAMBLE
PENTECOST

YOLH	=	HOLY
SEJUS	=	JESUS
RITSPI	=	SPIRIT
ESAPSTLO	=	APOSTLES
EMRJAUESL	=	JERUSALEM
GINSAPEK	=	SPEAKING
ANLESGGUA	=	LANGUAGES
ENPSCOTTE	=	PENTECOST
TGNEUOS	=	TONGUES
EFRI	=	FIRE

Name:_____

The Body of Christ received an amazing gift at Pentecost—the Holy Spirit! With that gift came another gift—a new prayer language. Here are 10 words from this week's Bible lesson passage that need to be unscrambled. Are you up to the task?

UNSCRAMBLE
PENTECOST

YOLH = _____

SEJUS = _____

RITSPI = _____

ESAPSTLO = _____

EMRJAUESL = _____

GINSAPEK = _____

ANLESGGUA = _____

ENPSCOTTE = _____

TGNEUOS = _____

EFRI = _____

WEEK 6: THINK BIG!

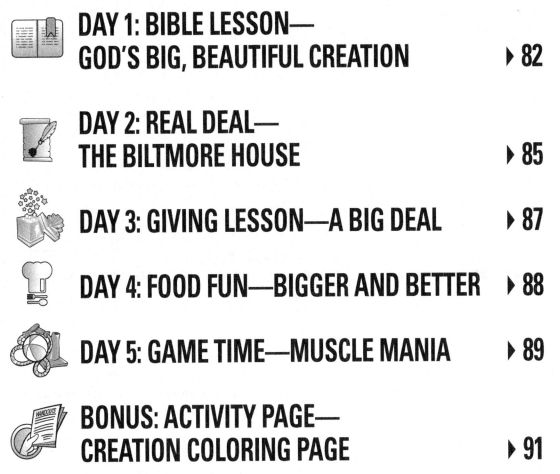
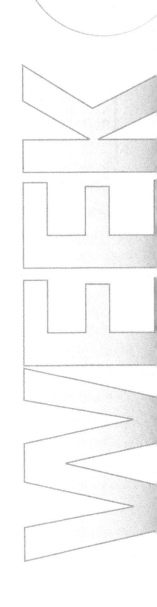

 Memory Verse: And we have received God's Spirit (not the world's spirit), so we can know the wonderful things God has freely given us. —1 Corinthians 2:12

WEEK 6: SNAPSHOT — THINK BIG!

DAY	TYPE OF LESSON	LESSON TITLE	SUPPLIES
Day 1	Bible Lesson	God's Big, Beautiful Creation	None
Day 2	Real Deal	The Biltmore House	Pictures of Biltmore House
Day 3	Giving Lesson	A Big Deal	Magnifying glass, Objects to "inspect"
Day 4	Food Fun	Bigger and Better	1 Medium-sized glass mixing bowl, Electric hand-held mixer, Measuring cups, 1 Large serving spoon, Plastic knife, Pie server, Small paper plates, Plastic forks, Napkins, Graham cracker pie crust, 1 Can lemon pie filling or lemon pudding mix, 1 Tablespoon meringue powder, Cold water, 6 Tablespoons +2 teaspoons sugar
Day 5	Game Time	Muscle Mania	2 Painter suits or adult-sized trench coats, Pink balloons, Blue balloons, Upbeat music (optional)
Bonus	Activity Page	Creation Coloring Page	1 Copy for each child

Lesson Introduction:

This is a great opportunity for a "think BIG" discussion. Ask kids to take a minute, close their eyes, and think of something really big they could do with their lives. Encourage them to share their BIG dreams, and challenge them to live big for Jesus. This isn't unreasonable when we realize that God loves us and created us to love Him and serve others.

Challenge your children to be part of a generation that will exchange God's thoughts for its own, self-serving thoughts. First Corinthians 2:16 and Isaiah 55:7, 11, offer us insight into God's thoughts. It's vital that we combat and overcome the religious idea that God's thoughts are not only higher but inaccessible to us. Your children *can* know God's thoughts, and they *can* be people of action and passion for Him!

Love,

Commander Dana

Commander Dana

Lesson Outline:

God is a big thinker. He has used His creativity to make this beautiful planet and everyone and everything in it. This week, encourage your children to be big thinkers too—to think outside of the typical and mundane. Challenge them to ask God to give them big dreams of accomplishments they can do for Him.

I. OUR FATHER THINKS BIG

a. God created a BIG and beautiful planet for us to enjoy.

b. God was thinking BIG when He created us in His image. Genesis 1:26

c. Our Father thought BIG when He sacrificed His Son to save us. John 3:16

II. GOD WANTS HIS CHILDREN TO THINK BIG, TOO Genesis 1:28

a. Adam and Eve were given an entire planet to rule.

b. As soon as they thought small, ungodly thoughts, trouble came!

c. Jesus came so we could have a BIG, satisfying life! John 10:10

III. OUR FATHER WILL GIVE US THE DESIRES OF OUR HEARTS Psalm 37:4

a. The way we think determines what we become. Proverbs 23:7

b. With God, a small person becomes great. 1 Samuel 16:11-13

c. Our Father doesn't think small, and neither should His kids!

Notes: _____

_____

_____

_____

_____

_____

_____

_____

_____

_____

_____

DAY 1: BIBLE LESSON | **GOD'S BIG, BEAUTIFUL CREATION**

Memory Verse: *And we have received God's Spirit (not the world's spirit), so we can know the wonderful things God has freely given us.* —1 Corinthians 2:12

This week, you'll share with your children about the bigness of God—His ability to create something beautiful and majestic from what looked like nothing, with the substance of His faith (Hebrews 11:3). What's even better is that your children can know God. They can know His heart. Through Jesus, the Holy Spirit and His Word, God has made it possible for His children to know Him and His ways so that we can all—no matter our age— be people of action for Him!

Read Genesis 1:1-31:
The Account of Creation

In the beginning God created the heavens and the earth. The earth was formless and empty, and darkness covered the deep waters. And the Spirit of God was hovering over the surface of the waters.

Then God said, "Let there be light," and there was light. And God saw that the light was good. Then he separated the light from the darkness. God called the light "day" and the darkness "night."

And evening passed and morning came, marking the first day.

Then God said, "Let there be a space between the waters, to separate the waters of the heavens from the waters of the earth." And that is what happened. God made this space to separate the waters of the earth from the waters of the heavens. God called the space "sky."

And evening passed and morning came, marking the second day.

Then God said, "Let the waters beneath the sky flow together into one place, so dry ground may appear." And that is what happened. God called the dry ground "land" and the waters "seas." And God saw that it was good. Then God said, "Let the land sprout with vegetation—every sort of seed-bearing plant, and trees that grow seed-bearing fruit. These seeds will then produce the kinds of plants and trees from which they came." And that is what happened. The land produced vegetation—all sorts of seed-bearing plants, and trees with seed-bearing fruit. Their seeds produced plants and trees of the same kind. And God saw that it was good.

And evening passed and morning came, marking the third day.

Then God said, "Let lights appear in the sky to separate the day from the night. Let them be signs to mark the seasons, days, and years. Let these lights in the sky shine down on the earth." And that is what happened. God made two great lights—the larger one to govern the day, and the smaller one to govern the night. He also made the stars. God set these lights in the sky to light the earth, to govern the day and night, and to separate the light from the darkness. And God saw that it was good.

And evening passed and morning came, marking the fourth day.

Then God said, "Let the waters swarm with fish and other life. Let the skies be filled with birds of every kind." So God created great sea creatures and every living thing that scurries and swarms in the water, and every sort of bird—each producing offspring of the same kind. And God saw that it was good. Then God blessed them, saying, "Be fruitful and multiply. Let the fish fill the seas, and let the birds multiply on the earth."

And evening passed and morning came, marking the fifth day.

Then God said, "Let the earth produce every sort of animal, each producing offspring of the same kind—livestock, small animals that scurry along the ground, and wild animals." And that is what happened. God made all sorts of wild animals, livestock, and small animals, each able to produce offspring of the same kind. And God saw that it was good.

Then God said, "Let us make human beings in our image, to be like us. They will reign over the fish in the sea, the birds in the sky, the livestock, all the wild animals on the earth, and the small animals that scurry along the ground."

So God created human beings in his own image.

In the image of God he created them; male and female he created them.

Then God blessed them and said, "Be fruitful and multiply. Fill the earth and govern it. Reign over the fish in the sea, the birds in the sky, and all the animals that scurry along the ground."

Then God said, "Look! I have given you every seed-bearing plant throughout the earth and all the fruit trees for your food. And I have given every green plant as food for all the wild animals, the birds in the sky, and the small animals that scurry along the ground—everything that has life." And that is what happened.

Then God looked over all he had made, and he saw that it was very good!

And evening passed and morning came, marking the sixth day.

Discussion Questions:

1. **What happened in this passage?**

   God created space, the earth and every living thing, including man and woman.

2. **How did God use His imagination during Creation?**

   He used His imagination to make all these things—the universe, plants, animals and people from what looked like nothing—through the substance of His faith. That's creative!

3. **Did that require Him to think big, beyond what was "normal"?**

   Absolutely! God had to think very, very BIG.

4. **Do you think God wants us to think big?**

   Yes, God wants to show us great things and help us do them. He needs us to think beyond what we see right in front of us so we can be obedient and do the big things He has for us to do.

5. **How do you think God shares His dreams with us?**

   If we'll listen, God will speak to us through the Bible, other people and by His Holy Spirit. It requires us to get to know Him by talking to Him, studying the Bible and listening to the Holy Spirit who lives inside our spirits.

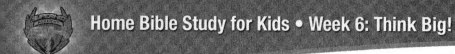
6. **Has God given you any dreams of things for you to do?**

   Parents, talk to your children about their dreams, understanding that God may very well be leading them, even in their young ages, to do specific things for Him. This is also a great time to talk about the dreams and plans God has given you, both past and present.

7. **Will you pray with me about the dreams God has given us?**

   Parents, pray as a family for God to fulfill His plans for your children.

Notes: _____

_____

_____

_____

_____

_____

_____

_____

_____

_____

_____

_____

_____

_____

_____

_____

_____

_____

_____

_____

_____

_____

_____

_____

_____

_____

_____

_____

DAY 2: REAL DEAL — THE BILTMORE HOUSE

 Memory Verse: *And we have received God's Spirit (not the world's spirit), so we can know the wonderful things God has freely given us.* —1 Corinthians 2:12

 Concept: Highlighting an interesting historical place, figure or event that illustrates the theme of the day. The theme of the day is asking God to help us think BIG!

Supplies: ■ Pictures of Biltmore House (available online)

Intro:

Today, we're focusing on big thinking, and as we've learned, no one thinks bigger than God! In our lesson, we will be learning about a man named George Vanderbilt.

Lesson:

Can someone say our Bible memory verse without looking at your Bible? *(Allow children to recite the verse.)* The Holy Spirit who is God's very own Spirit, lives inside us. He is the One who helps us think BIG and to believe Him to help us get it done!

About George Vanderbilt:

George Vanderbilt was a big thinker. Born in 1862, in New York City, George was the youngest of eight children born into one of the richest families in America—which gave him many opportunities to travel all over the world.

George loved to read, and by the age of 10, he had his own art and book collection. He read about 81 books every year. All this reading and education helped stir up George's imagination.

A BIG Idea—Biltmore House:

George had a BIG dream. He wanted to design and build the biggest house in America. He grew up in a 58-room mansion in Manhattan, New York, but George wanted an even bigger house. He wanted his mansion to be called the "Biltmore House," and it was to be located in the beautiful Blue Ridge Mountains of North Carolina. When he was 25 years old, George set to work, and after six years, the Biltmore House, his huge mansion, was nearly completed. *(Show children the pictures of the Biltmore House.)*

How BIG Is It?

George wanted the house to be special, so he bought 125,000 acres and built the house on that property. Along with his architect friend, Richard Morris Hunt, the two men's vision included a 250-room house that was

175,000 square feet inside. That's about the size of 88 normal-sized houses! George and his friend, Richard, ended up using more than 11 million bricks to complete the house. But, they couldn't just have a house in the middle of all that land. George wanted to have beautiful gardens and elegant landscaping surrounding his amazing four-story, 250-room French Renaissance chateau. So, he got a famous landscape designer named Fredrick Law Olmsted to design the elegant grounds that surround the Biltmore estate.[4]

Modern Advances:

George was constantly learning from inventors and engineers about incorporating modern amenities. Some modern advances George was able to use in this house included: electricity, fire alarms, elevators, intercoms, a pool, a bowling alley and much more. Now, that's thinking BIG!

Making History:

The Biltmore House is still owned by the Vanderbilt family and about a million tourists visit the house each year. It is still the biggest private residence in America and was officially named a National Historic Landmark.

Outro:

We can ask God to help us think big and discover creative ways to help others. What a BIG God we serve, and what an honor it is to journey through our lives trusting and relying on Him! George Vanderbilt followed through on his BIG dream, and God can help *us* live *our* big dreams and ideas. With His help and direction, we can do great things for Him.

It's true that no one can think bigger than God. He thought up the whole world, people and animals! But, George Vanderbilt certainly thought big when he built America's largest, most amazing home. That's why he and the Biltmore House are today's Real Deal.

---

4 "Biltmore Estate and George Vanderbilt History," Romantic Asheville, Insider's Guide to the NC Mountains, http://www.romanticashe-ville.com/biltmorececil.htm (4/19/16).

Notes: _____

_____

_____

_____

_____

_____

_____

_____

_____

_____

_____

DAY 3: GIVING LESSON

A BIG DEAL

Suggested Time: 10 minutes

Offering Scripture: Let the Lord be magnified, Who takes pleasure in the prosperity of His servant. —Psalm 35:27b AMPC

Supplies: ■ Magnifying glass, ■ Objects to "inspect" such as bugs, rocks or plants

Lesson Instructions:

Has anyone ever used a magnifying glass? Can you tell me what a magnifying glass is used for? Yes! You're right. A magnifying glass is used to help us see things that are small. Tiny details become much bigger and easier to observe with the help of a magnifying glass.

I have a magnifying glass right here. I'm going to let each of you use it to inspect these objects. Can you tell me what you see? *(Allow time for observation and discussion.)*

We have a really cool scripture today. It's from Psalm 35:27b in *The Amplified Bible, Classic Edition:* "Let the Lord be *magnified,* Who takes pleasure in the prosperity of His servant."

This scripture teaches us about magnifying or exalting God. Wow! We've already talked about what it means to magnify something—to enlarge or make it even bigger. To *exalt* means "to honor, praise or glorify." This verse is telling us to make a big deal of our praise and worship to our wonderful heavenly Father.

God is so great and so amazing that He deserves our praise. We have the opportunity to take pleasure in worshiping Him!

The second part of this verse teaches us that God is happy when we are living lives that are pleasing to Him and when we are prospering. He is pleased when we have more than enough to eat, more than enough clothes to wear, and we're BLESSED! When we live to love God and others, we are fulfilling God's greatest commandment. He delights to bless us.

Giving is a way that we show God just how thankful we are for all He has given us. So let's express our love and thankfulness to God right now by preparing our offerings for Him.

Notes: _____

_____

_____

_____

_____

_____

DAY 4: FOOD FUN — BIGGER AND BETTER

Suggested Time: 10 minutes

Memory Verse: And we have received God's Spirit (not the world's spirit), so we can know the wonderful things God has freely given us. —1 Corinthians 2:12

Teacher Tip: Meringue powder can be found in most craft and home decor stores or any store that sells cake decorating supplies. It's a good alternate to using raw egg whites.

Ingredients: ☐ 1 Graham cracker pie crust, ☐ 1 Can lemon pie filling or lemon pudding mix, ☐ 1 Tablespoon meringue powder, ☐ 1/4 Cup cold water, ☐ 6 Tablespoons + 2 teaspoons sugar

Supplies: ■ 1 Medium glass mixing bowl, ■ Electric hand-mixer, ■ Measuring cups, ■ 1 Large serving spoon, ■ Plastic knife, ■ Pie server, ■ Small paper plates, ■ Plastic forks, ■ Napkins, ■ Graham cracker pie crust, ■ 1 Can lemon pie filling or lemon pudding mix, ■ Meringue powder, ■ Cold water, ■ Sugar

Prior to Lesson:

For simplicity, prepare the topping beforehand. You can keep the topping's ingredients on the counter so your children can see what you used. Emphasize how something small can become something big.

Prepare meringue and graham cracker crust according to package directions included on the meringue powder container and graham cracker crust package. Bake the pie crust. Refrigerate the meringue and pie crust so it can be chilled for your lesson.

During lesson, use a spoon to pile meringue high on top of the pie filling; the more topping, the better. Remember, your lesson is all about thinking big like God!

Lesson Instructions:

Today, you're going to help me make dessert for tonight's dinner! We'll be taking an ordinary lemon pie and turning it into something BIG and special.

This meringue powder reminds me of our thoughts. Sometimes, we get so involved in thinking about ourselves, our thoughts can look like this meringue powder—small and flat.

When we focus on loving God and asking Him to show us ways to bless others, we are thinking big and creatively, just like He does!

So let's put this yummy pie together. Can you see how big the pie gets when we keep adding the meringue? *(Pile the lemon pie filling, then the meringue into the graham cracker crust.)* That's just like adding good God-thoughts to our lives. The more we think on good things, the more we live and experience good things! *(Bake the pie to brown the meringue topping before eating.)*

DAY 5: GAME TIME | **MUSCLE MANIA**

 Suggested Time: *8-10 minutes*

 Memory Verse: *And we have received God's Spirit (not the world's spirit), so we can know the wonderful things God has freely given us.* —1 Corinthians 2:12

 Teacher Tip: *Present the memory verse to your children and allow them to repeat it several times. Include your own hand gestures and movements to help them remember it more easily.*

Supplies: ■ *2 Painter suits or adult-sized trench coats,* ■ *20 balloons (divided into two groups),* ■ *Upbeat music to play during activity (optional)*

Prior to Game:

Place 10 balloons next to 1 painter suit (or trench coat) and 10 balloons next to the other painter suit (or trench coat).

Game Instructions:

Divide players into 2 teams. Select 2 players to be the "muscle" for each team. Those players will wear the painter suits or coats.

When the game starts, the other players will blow up the balloons and stuff them into the suit to make it look like muscles.

Game Goal:

The first team to blow up 10 balloons, place them in the suit and zip it, wins!

Final Word:

As today's memory verse states, "And we have received God's Spirit (not the world's spirit), so we can know the wonderful things God has freely given us." We can see from the first part of this chapter in 1 Corinthians, that God has big thoughts and plans for us. We can always expect Him to have BIG, creative ideas to help us!

In our game, we worked as a team to create muscle men or muscle women. Muscle men and women have to exercise long and hard to help their muscles grow BIG.

But with God, His thoughts for us are not just big, but HUGE! And, we don't have to work hard to receive them. He's given us His Spirit so we can know all the wonderful things He has freely given us. Muscle men and women may *think* they're big, but with God, we *are* big!

Variation No 1: Younger Players

For younger players who are unable to safely blow up balloons, have the balloons already blown up. The teams can still race to fill the muscle man/woman with balloons. The first team to insert all 10 balloons, wins.

Variation No 2: Small Groups

For families with only 1 or 2 children, have Dad or Mom wear the suit and time the children to see who can make Dad or Mom into a muscle man/woman. Children can even race against themselves by seeing if they can beat their previous times.

Notes: _____

_____

_____

_____

_____

_____

_____

_____

_____

_____

_____

_____

_____

_____

_____

_____

_____

_____

_____

_____

_____

_____

_____

_____

WEEK 7: IT'S TRUE

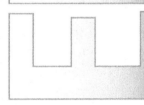
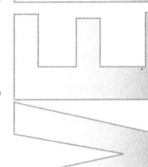

Memory Verse: And you will know the truth, and the truth will set you free. —John 8:32

WEEK 7 SNAPSHOT — IT'S TRUE

DAY	TYPE OF LESSON	LESSON TITLE	SUPPLIES
Day 1	Bible Lesson	The Choice of Life or Death	None
Day 2	Read-Aloud	The Truth Will Make You Free	None
Day 3	Giving Lesson	The Giving Experiment	10 $1 bills, Small notepad, Pen
Day 4	Object Lesson	Cheese and Crackers	Crackers, Cheese slices, Serving platter
Day 5	Game Time	Truth Quick-Draw	2 Pingpong paddles, Paint stirring sticks or signs with handles, Small prizes, 1 Large prize
Bonus	Activity Page	Recognizing Truth Word Search	1 Copy for each child

Lesson Introduction:

The more we learn about God and His love for us, the more we'll want to live lives that represent truth and freedom. God's Word says we reap what we sow, and we want to sow good seeds into our hearts and the hearts of others. It honors our Father when we are truthful, and living that way allows us to bring life to others.

Let's agree in prayer together and ask God to help us recognize His truth, and allow the Holy Spirit to guide us into truth and understanding as we guide our children.

Love,

Commander Dann

Commander Kellie

Lesson Outline:

This week, your children will be reminded of the difference between God's truth and the devil's lies. The enemy will lie and try to destroy them, but God never will. His way *always* leads to healing and love.

I. GOD IS TRUTH Deuteronomy 32:4

a. God wants our lives to be full of truth. Psalm 51:6

b. To see truth, we should look at Jesus! John 14:6

c. The Holy Spirit leads us to truth. John 16:13

II. THE DEVIL HAS NO TRUTH IN HIM John 8:44

a. We live in a world where lying is common.

b. Satan is the father of lies—he started lying and has not stopped!

c. Keeping our eyes on Jesus will keep truth and honesty before us.

III. TRUTH AND FREEDOM GO TOGETHER John 8:32

a. Lying and dishonesty bring bondage, but truth brings freedom and joy!

b. Choosing truth is choosing life. Deuteronomy 30:19

c. Our Father wants His kids to be free, free, free!

Notes: _____

_____

_____

_____

_____

_____

_____

_____

_____

_____

_____

_____

DAY 1: BIBLE LESSON THE CHOICE OF LIFE OR DEATH

 Memory Verse: And you will know the truth, and the truth will set you free. —John 8:32

You're talking to your children this week about seeking truth. The world and the enemy will try to convince them that truth is subjective, but we know God's truth is absolute. His Word teaches us to know and understand His truth. Being able to differentiate between the world's truth and God's truth determines how fulfilling and honorable our lives will be.

Read Deuteronomy 30:15-20:
The Choice of Life or Death

Now listen! Today I am giving you a choice between life and death, between prosperity and disaster. For I command you this day to love the Lord your God and to keep his commands, decrees, and regulations by walking in his ways. If you do this, you will live and multiply, and the Lord your God will bless you and the land you are about to enter and occupy.

But if your heart turns away and you refuse to listen, and if you are drawn away to serve and worship other gods, then I warn you now that you will certainly be destroyed. You will not live a long, good life in the land you are crossing the Jordan to occupy.

Today I have given you the choice between life and death, between blessings and curses. Now I call on heaven and earth to witness the choice you make. Oh, that you would choose life, so that you and your descendants might live! You can make this choice by loving the Lord your God, obeying him, and committing yourself firmly to him. This is the key to your life. And if you love and obey the Lord, you will live long in the land the Lord swore to give your ancestors Abraham, Isaac, and Jacob.

Discussion Questions:

1. **What does this passage tell us?**

   This passage tells us that <u>we</u> can choose life or death. Following God's ways leads to life, but following the world's ways always leads to death.

2. **What examples does this passage give us for following God's ways?**

   We love God by obeying Him and committing ourselves to Him.

3. **How can we know how to obey God?**

   We know how to obey God by reading His Word and obeying what it says, as well as praying and listening to the Holy Spirit inside our spirits.

4. **What examples does this passage give us for the world's ways?**

   The world's ways include turning away from the Lord and serving and worshiping other gods.

5. **What does God promise us if we obey and honor Him?**

   He promises to bless us.

6. **What does God promise if we disobey Him?**

   We'll not live a good life. Life will be hard for us.

Notes: _____

_____

_____

_____

_____

_____

_____

_____

_____

_____

_____

_____

_____

_____

_____

_____

_____

_____

_____

_____

_____

_____

_____

_____

_____

_____

_____

DAY 2: READ-ALOUD

THE TRUTH WILL MAKE YOU FREE

 Suggested Time: 15 minutes

 Memory Verse: And you will know the truth, and the truth will set you free. —John 8:32

Background:

This story focuses on the importance of telling the truth.

Story:

Ty sat at the table playing cards with his mom. Usually, his mom won, but today was Ty's day. He was up by 100 points and needed one card to go out. His mom, on the other hand, was sitting across from him with a handful of cards and a tense look on her face. With every card she drew, she let out a sound of disgust. "Ugh." Then she discarded the worthless card. Thankfully, everything she discarded, Ty picked up. She'd been feeding him good cards all afternoon.

Finally, she threw down the king of hearts—just the card Ty needed. He grabbed it and threw his run down. "Boom! Who's the champion now?"

"You did it! You beat me fair and square. Congratulations, Champ!"

"I can't believe it. I *never* win," Ty said, marveling at the turn of events.

"You've become quite a card player. I'm impressed," his mom said, standing and ruffling his hair. "Now, it's time for dinner." She made her way to the refrigerator, opened it and began searching inside.

"What are we having?" Ty asked, as he gathered the cards and returned them to the card box.

"Your favorite—Dad's barbecue, left over from the cookout."

Ty froze and looked at his mom. "Um, I don't think that's gonna work."

"What do you mean? You love your dad's left over barbecue. And I love not having to cook dinner."

Ty cringed. "I just, uh, don't think there's any left."

His mom stopped, shut the door and turned to him. "What do you mean? There was a whole pan of chicken left over. There should be plenty for dinner tonight and maybe even enough for your father's lunch tomorrow."

"Well, uh, I kind of ate it," he confessed quietly.

"Excuse me?"

Ty coughed. "I ate it."

"All of it?"

"Yes, ma'am."

"When?" she asked.

"Last night. I got really hungry after my soccer game."

"OK, well, we still have some sides." His mom opened the refrigerator again and began moving containers around, looking for the sides.

"Um, well…"

"You ate those too?" she asked, closing the door.

"Yes, ma'am."

"Ty!"

"I was hungry, Mom. I needed a snack."

"I guess so. You must have worked up quite an appetite." She smiled. "Next time, talk to me before you eat *all* the leftovers. I can't plan our meals if food disappears without me knowing about it."

"Yes, ma'am, I will. I'm sorry."

"I appreciate your being honest about it. You spoke up and told me the truth. I'm proud of you, and you know what? God's proud of you, too. You're an honorable young man." She walked toward him and ruffled his hair again and then smiled. "An honorable young man with a huge appetite, but an honorable young man."

Ty smiled back at her.

"Let's call your father and talk to him about going out to dinner. What sounds good?"

Ty stood up from the table. "Well, I've had enough barbecue, so how about Chinese?"

His mom laughed. "I'll bet you've had enough barbecue." Then she walked to the phone to call Ty's dad.

Discussion Questions:

1. **What happened in the story?**

   Ty had eaten the food his mother had planned to serve for dinner.

2. **Why was Ty's mother proud of him?**

   He was honest about eating all the leftovers, rather than trying to cover it up.

3. **Could he have lied? What do you think would have happened had he lied?**

   Yes, he could have acted like he didn't know what had happened to the food by staying quiet, but his mother probably would have figured out that someone had eaten the food.

4. Why is telling the truth so important?

It's honorable and shows maturity when we tell the truth. People know that they can trust us and that we won't look for an easy way out when things get tough.

5. Why does it matter to God that we tell the truth?

God wants to trust us, too. He wants to know that He can rely on us, and we won't try to hide or cover up when we make mistakes. That way He can trust us with more responsibility for His kingdom.

Notes: _____

_____

_____

_____

_____

_____

_____

_____

_____

_____

_____

_____

_____

_____

_____

_____

_____

_____

_____

_____

_____

_____

_____

_____

_____

_____

DAY 3: GIVING LESSON

THE GIVING EXPERIMENT

Suggested Time: 10 minutes

Offering Scripture: Give freely and spontaneously. Don't have a stingy heart. The way you handle matters like this triggers God, your God's, blessing in everything you do, all your work and ventures.
—Deuteronomy 15:10 MSG

Supplies: ■ 10 $1 bills, ■ Small notepad, ■ Pen

Lesson Instructions:

Today, our lesson involves money, more specifically, the money God gives us and how we handle it. The instructions for this lesson have to do with our scripture from Deuteronomy 15:10 (MSG), which says, "Give freely and spontaneously. Don't have a stingy heart. The way you handle matters like this triggers God, your God's, blessing in everything you do…."

I'm going to give you 10 $1 bills to give away throughout the coming week. You're free to give them in any way you choose, but I need you to write down how you choose to give each dollar.

I'm looking for details on where you gave, how much you gave, why you chose to give, and to whom—so keep track of it!

It'll be great to see how God helps you bless others with this money and the results of your giving. We'll talk about it next week!

Let's say our offering scripture together.

God cares about money and how we use it. We want to honor Him by being good stewards over all the blessings He gives us. Let's prepare our offering for this week's service.

Notes: _____

_____

_____

_____

_____

_____

_____

_____

_____

DAY 4: OBJECT LESSON — CHEESE & CRACKERS

 Suggested Time: 10 minutes

 Memory Verse: And you will know the truth, and the truth will set you free. —John 8:32

 Teacher Tip: This is a great object lesson to present right before dinner. Have your children come to the table and let them eat the cheese and crackers while you share the lesson. Then, when you've finished the lesson, you can present a delicious family meal. It will help show the difference between the cheese and crackers and the full meal that George missed.

Supplies: ■ Crackers, ■ Cheese slices, ■ Serving platter

Lesson Instructions:

Today, we'll be learning about a man who moved to America from the other side of the world. It was so long ago, that the only way to travel overseas was by boat, and that usually took several months.

George didn't have much money. It took most of his money to buy a boat ticket. He also needed food for his two-month trip on the boat to America, so he had just enough money left to stock up on cheese and crackers.

George was so excited to be on his way to America! The first thing he did was explore the boat. He passed by a big window that looked into a dining room. There was a huge buffet table full of delicious food—ham, turkey, baked potatoes, fruit, rolls and pies. All the people eating in the dining room sure looked happy! But, George still had plenty of cheese and crackers for his meals.

One week passed, and every day—breakfast, lunch and dinner—George ate cheese and crackers. Then two weeks passed, then three weeks, and finally the first month. Each week, day after day, George continued to eat cheese and crackers.

Passing by the dining room window was getting more challenging. Sometimes George stopped to stare at all the food until people started getting annoyed and waved at him to move on. He could almost taste the juicy turkey and baked potatoes. A few times, George dreamed he was eating in the dining room with all the other happy people. He even woke up chewing air.

After two months of his cheese-and-cracker routine, the day had finally come to land in America. The first thing George wanted was to find a good place to eat, and eat anything other than cheese and crackers!

He was leaning over the boat rail, looking out at the water, when the captain approached. The captain asked George how he had enjoyed the trip.

George shared with the captain that he was excited to get off the boat.

"But why? Didn't you like the boat?" asked the captain. George assured the captain that the boat was great; he just hadn't eaten very well.

The captain looked surprised by George's response. "Didn't you like the food in the dining room?"

George explained how he'd spent almost all of his money on the boat ticket, which left just enough money to buy cheese and crackers for all his meals.

"Didn't anyone tell you, the price of the ticket included all your food?"

George felt all the blood drain out of his face. He couldn't believe it! He quickly got out his ticket and read the fine print at the bottom. Sure enough, it said, "Meals included." George didn't know whether to cry, yell or jump overboard. He was so upset!

If only he had known the truth and read the fine print on his ticket!

This story is a good illustration of our memory verse today in John 8:32. When you know the truth, it sets you free.

When we seek God's truth and freedom found in His Word, we'll understand more and more in our hearts that God loves us and wants only good for our lives. He'll help us see the "fine print" and not miss the fulfilling opportunities He has for us.

Notes: _____

_____

_____

_____

_____

_____

_____

_____

_____

_____

_____

_____

_____

_____

_____

_____

_____

_____

_____

_____

_____

_____

DAY 5: GAME TIME — TRUTH QUICK-DRAW

 Suggested Time: 10-15 minutes

 Memory Verse: And you will know the truth, and the truth will set you free. —John 8:32

 Teacher Tip: Present the Memory Verse to your children, and allow them to repeat it several times. Include your own hand gestures and movements to help them remember it more easily.

Supplies: ■ 2 Pingpong paddles, painter's stir sticks or signs with handles, ■ Small prizes, ■ 1 Large prize

Prior to Game:

Using pingpong paddles, paint stirring sticks, or signs with handles, write or attach signs that read "True" on one side, and "False" on the other side.

Game Instructions:

It can be really challenging to recognize truth, but we can ask God and the Holy Spirit to help us in every situation.

We're going to play a game today in which we'll challenge each other to recognize statements that are true or false.

Whoever holds up the correct side of the paddle first, wins a point.

Let's line up right here. Each time I read a question or statement, if you know it's true, what are you going to do? Right! You'll hold up the "true" side. And, if you know the question or statement is false? Right again! Hold up the "false" side of the paddle sign.

Game Goal:

Challenge your children to recognize truth quickly. The person to win the most points wins a prize.

Final Word:

Recognizing truth is important. Jesus said in John 8:32, "And you will know the truth, and the truth will set you free." The more we keep our eyes on Jesus, loving Him and loving others, the easier it will be to identify truth when you see or hear it.

Variation No. 1: Dinner Choice

If you prefer not to give prizes, allow the winner to choose the dinner menu one night.

Variation No. 2: One Player

If you only have one child, play the game the same way, but give the child a point for each question he gets correct and give yourself a point for each question he gets wrong. You can even break the game into three heats of five questions each. So if he loses one heat, he still has a chance to win the next one.

Notes: _____

_____

_____

_____

_____

_____

_____

_____

_____

_____

_____

_____

_____

_____

_____

_____

_____

_____

_____

_____

_____

_____

_____

_____

_____

_____

DAY 5: GAME TIME CONT. TRUTH QUICK-DRAW:

TRUE OR FALSE QUESTIONS

1. Moses built the Ark exactly as God commanded.
   FALSE—<u>Noah</u> built the Ark. Genesis 6:13-14

2. Jesus was born in Nazareth.
   FALSE—Jesus was actually born in <u>Bethlehem</u>.
   Matthew 2:1

3. Isaac was born when Abraham was 100 years old.
   TRUE—Genesis 21:5

4. Faith comes by hearing the Word of God
   TRUE— Romans 10:17

5. Jesus multiplied five loaves and two fishes.
   TRUE—John 6:9-11

6. Joseph had 12 brothers.
   FALSE—Joseph had 11 brothers; including Joseph, that makes 12! Exodus 1:1-5

7. Peter paid his taxes by going fishing.
   TRUE—Matthew 17:24-27

8. The two most important commandments are to fast and pray.
   FALSE—Jesus said the greatest commandments are to love God and other people! Matthew 22:36-39

9. Shepherds came to see Jesus when He was born.
   TRUE—Luke 2:15-16

10. One of the fruit of the spirit is a banana.
    FALSE— Read Galatians 5:22-23.

11. Goliath was 6 cubits and a span. (Nearly 10 feet tall)
    TRUE—1 Samuel 17:4

12. Jesus did His first miracle for His mother.
    TRUE—John 2:1-11

13. Martha worked in the kitchen instead of listening to Jesus.
    TRUE—Luke 10:40-42

14. Jehoshaphat defeated an entire army with singing, praising God and music.
    TRUE—2 Chronicles 20:22

15. Isaac's firstborn son received his blessing.
    FALSE—Esau <u>sold his blessing</u> to his younger brother, Jacob. Genesis 25:30-33

16. One time, the Apostle Paul preached until someone fell out of a window and died.
    TRUE—Acts 20:9

17. The tithe is 5 percent of our income.
    FALSE—The tithe is 10 percent. Leviticus 27:30, 32

18. Three hundred men were in Gideon's army.
    TRUE—Judges 7:7

19. Five lepers thanked Jesus for healing them.
    FALSE—Only <u>one</u> said thanks! Luke 17:17

20. In the Bible, there is a donkey that talked.
    TRUE—Numbers 22:28

Notes: _____
_____
_____
_____
_____

ACTIVITY PAGE

RECOGNIZING TRUTH WORD SEARCH

 Memory Verse: And you will know the truth, and the truth will set you free. —John 8:32

ANSWER KEY:

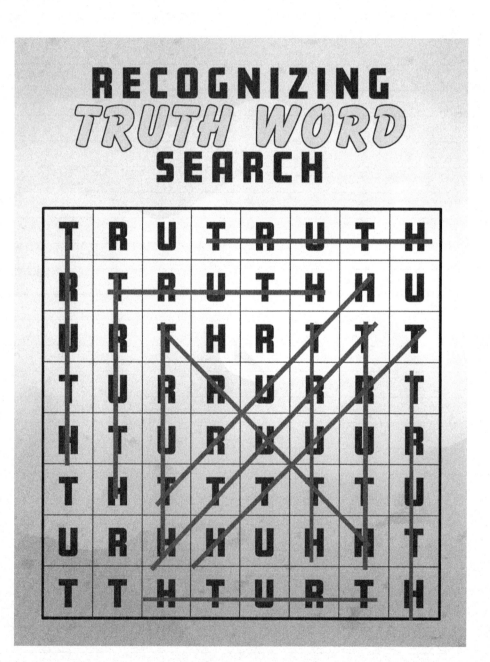

Name:_____

In this week's lesson, you learned about identifying God's truth. In this word search, the word TRUTH appears 13 times. See if you can identify every one. Look horizontally, vertically and diagonally.

RECOGNIZING
TRUTH WORD
SEARCH

T	R	U	T	R	U	T	H
R	T	R	U	T	H	H	U
U	R	T	H	R	T	T	T
T	U	R	R	U	R	R	T
H	T	U	R	U	U	U	R
T	H	T	T	T	T	T	U
U	R	H	H	U	H	H	T
T	T	H	T	U	R	T	H

Notes: _____

_____

_____

_____

_____

_____

_____

_____

_____

_____

_____

_____

_____

_____

_____

_____

_____

_____

_____

_____

_____

_____

_____

_____

_____

_____

_____

_____

_____

_____

_____

_____

_____

WEEK 8: GOD'S WORD NEVER CHANGES

 Memory Verse: But the word of the Lord remains forever. And that word is the Good News that was preached to you. —1 Peter 1:25

WEEK 8 SNAPSHOT

GOD'S WORD NEVER CHANGES

DAY	TYPE OF LESSON	LESSON TITLE	SUPPLIES
Day 1	Bible Lesson	Your Eternal Word	None
Day 2	Academy Lab	Things Are Changing	1/4 Cup white vinegar, 1/4 Teaspoon baking soda, Large, clear drinking glass, 1 Head of red cabbage, 1 Gallon distilled water, Saucepan, Sieve, 1 Spouted measuring cup, Spoon, Storage jar
Day 3	Giving Lesson	God and Sons	10 $1 Bills, 10 Dimes
Day 4	Food Fun	Depend on It	1 Glass pitcher, 1 Serving spoon, Hand-held citrus juicer, Drinking cups, 5 Cups ice water, 1/2 Cup sugar, 1 Cup hot water, 8 Lemons
Day 5	Game Time	Popcorn Pass	Popcorn (with no butter or salt), 2 Large bowls, 10 Popcorn "scoop" cups
Bonus	Activity Page	Your Eternal Word Crossword Puzzle	1 Copy for each child

Lesson Introduction:

Some people enjoy change and find it adventurous. For others, change is not easy or fun. Let's take a few moments and discuss things that change. (Example: trees, clothes, cars, the weather, and us!) Thanks to our heavenly Father, we can all trust in something that never changes—God's Word and His love for us!

Now let's take a few moments and thank God for His unconditional and never-ending love for us. He is the same yesterday, today and tomorrow. It's great to know our Father is always there for us!

Love,

Commander Dana

Commander Dana

Lesson Outline:

God's Word never changes. It is the same yesterday, today and forever, and the Bible refers to Jesus as the Word of God. This week, share this powerful truth with your children. God's Word—Jesus—remains unchanged. He is faithful and trustworthy!

I. THE WORD OF GOD NEVER CHANGES

a. God's Word stands forever. 1 Peter 1:25; Isaiah 40:8

b. It will never pass away or become outdated! Matthew 24:35

c. Our Father wants His kids to count on His Word. He keeps it!

II. WE CAN TRUST OUR HEAVENLY FATHER

a. Our Father is faithful. He is with us always. Psalm 119:90

b. God's Word reaches generation after generation. Psalm 119:90

c. God never changes. Malachi 3:6

III. JESUS IS CALLED "THE WORD OF GOD" Revelation 19:11-13

a. God's Word (Jesus!) never fails. Luke 16:17

b. God's Word (Jesus!) gave His life for us. John 3:16

c. God's Word (Jesus!) teaches us to trust and believe in Him. John 14:1

Notes: _____

_____

_____

_____

_____

_____

_____

_____

_____

_____

DAY 1: BIBLE LESSON YOUR ETERNAL WORD

 Memory Verse: *But the word of the Lord remains forever. And that word is the Good News that was preached to you.* —1 Peter 1:25

God's Word is eternal! It stands the test of time. This week's lesson focuses on the importance of God's Word. Your children (and you!) can rely on it. It will not let you down!

Read Psalm 119:89-96:

Your eternal word, O Lord, stands firm in heaven.

Your faithfulness extends to every generation, as enduring as the earth you created.

Your regulations remain true to this day, for everything serves your plans.

If your instructions hadn't sustained me with joy, I would have died in my misery.

I will never forget your commandments, for by them you give me life.

I am yours; rescue me! For I have worked hard at obeying your commandments.

Though the wicked hide along the way to kill me, I will quietly keep my mind on your laws.

Even perfection has its limits, but your commands have no limit.

Discussion Questions:

1. **What does it mean when it says God's Word "stands firm in heaven"?**

   God's Word is honored and upheld in heaven for all eternity.

2. **The next line says, "Your faithfulness extends to every generation, as enduring as the earth you created." What does that mean?**

   God's love is for everyone, throughout all time. He has never stopped loving or caring for mankind.

3. **Look at this verse: "I will never forget your commandments, for by them you give me life." How could God's commandment, His Word, give us life?**

   Jesus said in John 6:63 (KJV), "The words that I speak unto you, they are spirit, and they are life." God's words carry the power of God Himself. His *zoe,* or everlasting life, fills His words. They carry healing, deliverance, love, joy and peace. When we put them into our hearts, they bring God's life into our innermost being.

4. **Parents, talk to your children about what God's Word has meant to you. How has it affected your life? Is there a time when you received an answer to a problem or situation from God's Word?**

Notes: _____

_____

_____

_____

_____

_____

_____

_____

_____

_____

_____

_____

_____

_____

_____

_____

_____

_____

_____

_____

_____

_____

_____

_____

_____

_____

_____

_____

_____

_____

_____

DAY 2: ACADEMY LAB — THINGS ARE CHANGING

Suggested Time: *10 minutes*

Memory Verse: *But the word of the Lord remains forever. And that word is the Good News that was preached to you.* —1 Peter 1:25

Ingredients for Blue Brew: ☐ 1 Head of red cabbage, ☐ 1 Gallon distilled water

Recipe:
1. *Chop or shred the cabbage into small pieces. Place the cabbage in a saucepan.*
2. *Add enough distilled water to cover the cabbage. Simmer for about 20 minutes.*
3. *Let the cabbage cool for about 1/2 an hour.*
4. *Pour through a sieve and into a spouted measuring cup.*
5. *Use the back of a spoon to push out all liquid from the cabbage; then pour liquid into a storage jar.*

Supplies: ■ *Blue brew,* ■ *½ Cup white vinegar,* ■ *¼ Teaspoon baking soda,* ■ *Large, clear drinking glass,* ■ *1 Head of red cabbage,* ■ *1 Gallon distilled water,* ■ *Saucepan,* ■ *Sieve,* ■ *Spouted measuring cup,* ■ *Spoon,* ■ *Storage jar*

Prior to Lesson:

Prepare "Blue Brew."

Lesson Instructions:

Today, we'll be conducting an experiment using three main ingredients: Blue Brew, white vinegar and baking soda. I'll bet you're wondering, *What in the world is Blue Brew?* Has anyone ever seen an experiment that uses Blue Brew? I made the Blue Brew from boiling cabbage and getting the liquid out of it. Notice it's a bluish color.

Well, let's get started and find out what happens when these three ingredients are mixed together.

First, we'll fill this tall glass with about 1/4 cup of Blue Brew. Can everyone see it? Next, we'll add just enough vinegar to make the color change—about 1/4 cup.

Wow, did you see that? That's really cool! By adding vinegar to the Blue Brew, the color changed.

Can anyone guess what might happen when we add baking soda to the mixture? Yes! Adding the baking soda will cause the brew to change colors *again.* We'll add about 1/4 teaspoon of baking soda to reverse the color. Now, the brew turns back to blue!

Blue Brew causes our mixture to change, but this week we're talking about something that <u>never</u> changes. Can you tell me what it is?

Exactly! God's Word never changes. There are a lot of things in this world that change, but not God's Word.

And that's why we can rely on it. We have security knowing that what God told people in His Word thousands of years ago is the same for us today because God doesn't change. He is constant.

Because He *is* constant, we know His Word is constant, too. It's the same yesterday, today and forever because He is. Numbers 23:19 says, "God is not a man, so he does not lie….he does not change his mind. Has he ever spoken and failed to act? Has he ever promised and not carried it through?" The answer is no!

We can *always* trust God and His Word!

Notes: _____

_____

_____

_____

_____

_____

_____

_____

_____

_____

_____

_____

_____

_____

_____

_____

_____

_____

_____

_____

_____

_____

_____

_____

_____

_____

_____

DAY 3: GIVING LESSON

GOD AND SONS

Suggested Time: *10 minutes*

Offering Scripture: Bring all the tithes (the whole tenth of your income) into the storehouse, that there may be food in My house, and prove Me now by it, says the Lord of hosts, if I will not open the windows of heaven for you and pour you out a blessing, that there shall not be room enough to receive it. —Malachi 3:10 AMPC

Parent Tip: This is a great time to follow up on the Giving Lesson from last week. How did your children distribute the money you gave them? What was the response? Did God move in a specific way? Did the Holy Spirit speak to them or impress them to do something specific? Discuss this and encourage them to be good stewards of the resources God has given them.

Supplies: ■ 10 $1 Bills, ■ 10 Dimes

Lesson Instructions:

Hey, Cadets! Today, we'll be discussing how to be a good business partner. You may be thinking, *Business partner? How can I be a business partner? I'm just a kid!*

Well, you're never too young to go into business with God!

Let's read our scripture together from Malachi 3:10: "Bring all the tithes (the whole tenth of your income) into the storehouse, that there may be food in My house, and prove Me now by it, says the Lord of hosts, if I will not open the windows of heaven for you and pour you out a blessing, that there shall not be room enough to receive it."

Does anyone know what it means to *tithe?* A tithe is giving 1/10 of the money we earn back to God to honor and obey Him. He always blesses the rest of our money when we give Him the first 10 percent. Today, I brought some money to demonstrate this principle.

Here's the first example: Say you took out the trash this week to help around the house, and I paid you $1.

Here are 10 dimes, which is the same thing as $1. So, if I know there are 10 of these dimes in $1, and the tithe is 1/10 of $1, how much would the tithe of $1 be?

You're right! It would be one dime!

Here's another example: What if you saw your neighbor's yard was full of leaves, and you decided to bless your neighbor by raking his lawn? The neighbor was so thankful and appreciative that he decided to pay you $10! *(Count out the 10 $1 bills as a visual aid for the kids.)*

So, knowing that the tithe is a tenth, how much would the tithe of the $10 be?

Correct—$1!

All right, I think you're getting this! It's such a gift and honor to have God as our business partner, isn't it? As we seek and obey Him, He'll continue to pour out His goodness on our lives.

During the next two weeks, we'll continue to discuss how our lives and our relationship with God can grow as we partner with Him.

Now, let's prepare our offering for this week's service.

Notes: _____

_____

_____

_____

_____

_____

_____

_____

_____

_____

_____

_____

_____

_____

_____

_____

_____

_____

_____

_____

_____

_____

_____

_____

_____

_____

_____

_____

_____

_____

_____

_____

DAY 4: FOOD FUN

DEPEND ON IT

 Suggested Time: 10 minutes

 Memory Verse: But the word of the Lord remains forever. And that word is the Good News that was preached to you. —1 Peter 1:25

 Ingredients for Simple Syrup and Lemon Juice: ☐ 1 Cup hot water, ☐ 1/2 Cup sugar, ☐ 8 Lemons

Recipe:

1. To make simple syrup, stir 1/2 cup of sugar into the cup of hot water. Let the sugar completely dissolve.

2. Squeeze the lemons into a measuring cup. Use a citrus juicer, if you have one.

Supplies: ☐ 1 Glass pitcher, ☐ 1 Serving spoon, ☐ Hand-held citrus juicer, ☐ Drinking cups, ☐ 5 Cups ice water, ☐ ½ Cup sugar, ☐ 1 Cup hot water, ☐ 8 Lemons

Prior to Lesson:

Prepare simple syrup and lemon juice.

Lesson Instructions:

Who can tell me the name of someone who never changes? Yes, you're right! It's God. He never changes. He is always there for us, always loving us and always willing to help us. His Word never changes, and we can put our trust in Him and what He says.

Today, we'll be conducting an experiment about change. Let's state a few things that are certain: God is good and wants the best for our lives; God never changes, and we are certain that if we tasted this sugar, it would be sweet, right?

How about lemons?

If we were to cut one open and squeeze some juice into our mouths, it would be pretty sour, right? So, we know that sugar is always sweet and lemons are always sour. Well, let's do a little experiment that will change the sweetness of the sugar and the sourness of the lemon juice. *(Follow simple syrup recipe, combine with pre-squeezed lemon juice, add it to the ice water, and present lemonade!)*

Since we added lemon juice, which is sour, and sugar, which is sweet, we were able to create a drink that is both sweet and sour. The sweetness of the sugar didn't change and the sourness of the lemon juice didn't change, but when combined, the flavors changed to form a delicious drink.

Flavors may change, but God and His Word never change. He always will remain the same. He is the BEST ingredient in our lives!

Notes: _____

_____

_____

_____

_____

_____

_____

_____

_____

_____

_____

_____

_____

_____

_____

_____

_____

_____

_____

_____

_____

_____

_____

_____

_____

_____

_____

DAY 5: GAME TIME — **POPCORN PASS**

 Suggested Time: 5-10 minutes

 Memory Verse: But the word of the Lord remains forever. And that word is the Good News that was preached to you. —1 Peter 1:25

 Parent Tip: Present the memory verse to your children and allow them to repeat it several times. Include your own hand gestures and movements to help them remember it more easily.

Supplies: ☐ Popcorn (with no butter or salt), ☐ 2 Large bowls, ☐ 10 Popcorn "scoop" cups

Prior to Game:

Prepare popcorn and separate into 2 large bowls.

Game Instructions:

Divide participants into 2 teams. Line up each team to form a straight line. Each player will receive a popcorn cup and hold the cup on top of his/her head. Players will remain in this position for the duration of the game. A moderator or parent will fill the first player's cup with popcorn.

Once the game begins, the first player will pour the popcorn from his/her cup into the cup of the player behind, all while keeping the cup firmly in place on top of his/her head—and so on, down the line. If there are only two players on each team, then pour the popcorn back and forth between the players 10 times.

Game play will continue until all players have caught and poured the popcorn.

Game Goal:

Players try to transport as much popcorn as possible from player to player. The team with the most popcorn remaining in the last cup, wins!

Final Word:

The amount of popcorn in the cups changed from start to finish, but God's Word and His love for us *never* change.

Variation No. 1: Kids vs. Parents

If your family has fewer players, then have the children play against their parents. Or, have one parent on each team.

Variation No. 2: Place to Place

If there are not enough participants to play a relay, then have the players race to transport popcorn from one location to another *(use bowls or boxes to distinguish start and finish locations).* The player who transports his/her popcorn with the fastest time, wins.

Variation No. 3: Beat Yourself

For players with different skill levels, or for only one player, have each player compete against himself or herself. Time each run to determine if the player can beat his/her own time.

Notes: _____

_____

_____

_____

_____

_____

_____

_____

_____

_____

_____

_____

_____

_____

_____

_____

_____

_____

_____

_____

_____

_____

_____

_____

ACTIVITY PAGE

YOUR ETERNAL WORD CROSSWORD PUZZLE

Memory Verse: *But the word of the Lord remains forever. And that word is the Good News that was preached to you.* —1 Peter 1:25

ANSWER KEY:

1 GENERATION
2 INSTRUCTION
3 REGULATION
4 WICKED
5 RESCUE
6 ETERNAL
7 LAWS
8 PERFECTION
9 COMMANDMENT
10 MISERY
YOUR
ETERNAL WORD
CROSSWORD PUZZLE

Name:_____

In this week's Bible Lesson (Psalm 119:89-96), you read about the importance of God's Word. Using words from that passage, complete the below crossword puzzle. A list of the answers is provided.

YOUR ETERNAL WORD CROSSWORD PUZZLE

WORDS

ETERNAL
GENERATION
REGULATION
INSTRUCTION
MISERY
RESCUE
COMMANDMENT
WICKED
LAWS
PERFECTION

ACROSS

1. AN ENTIRE GROUP OF PEOPLE WHO WERE BORN AROUND THE SAME TIME

5. TO FREE OR SAVE

6. HAVING NO BEGINNING OR END; LASTING ALWAYS AND FOREVER

9. ONE OF 10 LAWS GIVEN TO MOSES BY GOD

DOWN

2. THE ACT OF GIVING KNOWLEDGE; TEACHING

3. A RULE OR LAW THAT CONTROLS OR DIRECTS PEOPLE'S ACTIONS

4. EVIL IN ACTIONS OR IDEAS

7. THE SET OF RULES THAT PEOPLE IN A SOCIETY MUST FOLLOW

8. THE STATE OR CONDITION OF BEING WITHOUT A FAULT OR MISTAKE

10. A CONDITION IN WHICH ONE IS VERY UNHAPPY OR SUFFERS VERY MUCH

Notes: _____

_____

_____

_____

_____

_____

_____

_____

_____

_____

_____

_____

_____

_____

_____

_____

_____

_____

_____

_____

_____

_____

_____

_____

_____

_____

_____

_____

_____

_____

_____

_____

WEEK 9: IT'S ALIVE!

 Memory Verse: For the word of God is alive and powerful. It is sharper than the sharpest two-edged sword.
—Hebrews 4:12a

WEEK 9 SNAPSHOT — IT'S ALIVE!

DAY	TYPE OF LESSON	LESSON TITLE	SUPPLIES
Day 1	Bible Lesson	Children of Light	None
Day 2	Read-Aloud	Timmy and Jimmy: It's Alive!	None
Day 3	Giving Lesson	The Open Window	Single-serving-sized bags of pretzels
Day 4	Object Lesson	Chew It Up	1 Banana, 1 Baby bib
Day 5	Game Time	"Nothing but Net" Sword Drill	1 Laundry basket, 1 Roll masking tape, 1 Beach ball, 2 Bibles, Small prizes
Bonus	Activity Page	Unruly Roman Roads	1 Copy for each child

Lesson Introduction:

Words are powerful. We have the choice to use words that honor God and bring life to others, or use words that are mean and hurtful. Of course, as Christians, we want to live powerful lives for God—lives that create good things and bring joy to those around us. To do so we must have our words line up with the goal of our lives. Good words are a big part of a good life.

This is a perfect opportunity to have your Superkids practice speaking words that contain life. Give them examples like: "I'm glad you're in my family." Or, "Is there anything I can help you with today?" And, "We can pray together and God will answer us." Now, that's talking like God talks!

Love,

Commander Dana

Lesson Outline:

God's words are powerful, and so are ours. Our words can either share God's love, or they can hurt and destroy. This week, encourage your children to pay attention to their words. May every word they speak honor the Lord.

I. GOD IS LIGHT AND HE IS LIFE John 1:3-5

    a. We were created to be alive, like God. Ephesians 4:24

    b. Everything that has life in it came from God.

    c. God wants His kids to have the best life you can imagine! John 10:10

II. WORDS ARE EXTREMELY POWERFUL Hebrews 4:12

    a. God created everything we see with His Word. Genesis 1

    b. Plants, animals and people came alive because of God's words!

III. LIFE WORDS OR DEATH WORDS: WE GET TO CHOOSE Deuteronomy 30:15

    a. Our words contain life or death in them. Proverbs 18:21

    b. God's words are life-giving. Proverbs 4:22

    c. Choosing godly words is like getting a "life sentence"!

Notes: _____

_____

_____

_____

_____

_____

_____

_____

_____

_____

_____

DAY 1: BIBLE LESSON — CHILDREN OF LIGHT

Memory Verse: *For the word of God is alive and powerful. It is sharper than the sharpest two-edged sword.* —Hebrews 4:12a

Last week, you taught your children that God's Word is true. It's through His words that He created this amazing world. Why is that important? Because life and death are found in words, and our words are no different. This week, you'll share the significance of the words your children speak. Throughout the week, remind your children to speak words of life, words that encourage, heal and empower those around them. It's an important part of being a disciple of Jesus.

Read Ephesians 4:17-32:
Living as Children of Light

With the Lord's authority I say this: Live no longer as the Gentiles do, for they are hopelessly confused. Their minds are full of darkness; they wander far from the life God gives because they have closed their minds and hardened their hearts against him. They have no sense of shame. They live for lustful pleasure and eagerly practice every kind of impurity.

But that isn't what you learned about Christ. Since you have heard about Jesus and have learned the truth that comes from him, throw off your old sinful nature and your former way of life, which is corrupted by lust and deception. Instead, let the Spirit renew your thoughts and attitudes. Put on your new nature, created to be like God—truly righteous and holy.

So stop telling lies. Let us tell our neighbors the truth, for we are all parts of the same body. And "don't sin by letting anger control you." Don't let the sun go down while you are still angry, for anger gives a foothold to the devil.

If you are a thief, quit stealing. Instead, use your hands for good hard work, and then give generously to others in need. Don't use foul or abusive language. Let everything you say be good and helpful, so that your words will be an encouragement to those who hear them.

And do not bring sorrow to God's Holy Spirit by the way you live. Remember, he has identified you as his own, guaranteeing that you will be saved on the day of redemption.

Get rid of all bitterness, rage, anger, harsh words, and slander, as well as all types of evil behavior. Instead, be kind to each other, tenderhearted, forgiving one another, just as God through Christ has forgiven you.

Discussion Questions:

1. **Sum up this passage. What is God's Word instructing us to do?**

   We are called to live like we are God's children. We're to act and speak in ways that please and honor Him instead of speaking like those who don't know Him.

2. **Why do our actions matter? Why can't we behave any way we want, as long as we're saved?**

   God calls us to live in truth, as examples of the work He has done in our lives. He has taken us from spiritual darkness to light. We now know the truth of what is good and lasting—and we can't go back to acting the way we did before we knew that. We will never find peace if we try to do that.

3. **Why do our words matter? Can we speak any way we want?**

   Again, the truth and life that God has given us should be represented in the words we speak.

4. **Can our words affect others? If so, how?**

   Yes, our words have power. They can either build others up or tear them down. They can heal, or they can wound. The choice is ours.

5. **Can our words affect us?**

   Yes, our words can affect our own lives for good or for evil. The choice is ours. If we constantly tear ourselves down with negativity and complaining, we will limit what we're able to accomplish. If we're constantly complaining and focusing on the things that are not right in ourselves, in our lives and in those around us, we will destroy our potential, our creativity and our relationships. We will deeply hinder what we're able to accomplish.

Notes: _____

_____

_____

_____

_____

_____

_____

_____

_____

_____

_____

_____

_____

_____

_____

_____

_____

_____

Home Bible Study for Kids • Week 9: It's Alive!

DAY 2: READ-ALOUD

TIMMY AND JIMMY: IT'S ALIVE!

Suggested Time: 15 minutes

Memory Verse: For the word of God is alive and powerful. It is sharper than the sharpest two-edged sword. —Hebrews 4:12a

Background:

This week, our Read-Aloud focuses, in a humorous way, on the supernatural, life-changing power of God's Word.

Story:

Summer vacation had begun, and Timmy was heading to his best friend Jimmy's house to invite him over. His family was having a backyard barbecue to celebrate the first day of summer vacation. The two boys had been best friends ever since they were 2 years old. They were in the same grade at the same school and even attended the same church, which made youth group even cooler. Of course, just because they were friends didn't mean they were the same. Not at all. In fact, Timmy and Jimmy were complete opposites, but somehow their friendship worked. Timmy was the logical one, while Jimmy was the dreamer. Timmy kept Jimmy grounded, and Jimmy helped Timmy see the possibilities in life.

Timmy walked up Jimmy's driveway and into the garage. "Hey, what are you doing?" he asked. Jimmy stood frozen in the middle of the garage, staring at his Bible which lay on the ground.

"Shush!" Jimmy held up his hand as if to stop Timmy from breaking his trance.

"What are you doing?"

"Quiet. Don't move."

Timmy paused and watched his friend. Then he shook his head "Jimmy, I already told you. You're never going to catch a fly with chopsticks. That only happens in the movies."

Jimmy lifted a fly swatter to Timmy without looking at him. "I don't have chopsticks, but I've already got him." A smashed fly was stuck to a fly swatter laying next to him.

"Gross!" Timmy said.

"Hey, can you hold this so I can concentrate?" He handed the fly swatter to his friend, still keeping his eyes fixed on the Bible that lay on the floor.

"So if you're not trying to Mr. Miyagi a fly[5], what are you doing? And why won't you look at me?"

Jimmy shrugged, still staring at the ground. "I knew you wouldn't understand."

"Understand what? I have no idea what in the world you're talking about." Timmy could feel the heat rising to his face.

"I'm talking about God's Word."

"Huh? What about God's Word?" Timmy asked, becoming even more frustrated.

"I just read Hebrews 4:12, and it says that God's Word is alive and powerful."

"So?"

Jimmy shook his head ever so slightly. Clearly, Timmy wasn't understanding a simple concept. "Alive means moving. And when my Bible moves, you can bet I'm gonna be here to see it. I even have my camera phone ready to prove it."

Timmy rolled his eyes. "First of all, that's not what Hebrews 4:12 means. And second, even if your Bible did move and you took a picture, that wouldn't prove anything. How would someone know it moved in a picture? It would just be a picture of a Bible."

Jimmy paused and turned to his friend. "Oh, I never thought of that. But I'm still not convinced about the first part. If my Bible's not gonna move, then why did God say it's alive?"

"God wasn't talking about the book and pages! He was talking about the *words* in the Bible. The words God spoke are full of life and can cause things to happen. That's why they're called alive and powerful."

Jimmy nodded his head. "I get that. It's kind of like me."

Squinting, Timmy asked, "How's that?"

"My mom says I'm always moving."

Timmy smiled. "I bet she does."

"So why did you come over, anyway?" Jimmy asked.

"I ask myself that all the time."

"What?"

"Never mind. You wanna come over to our house? My dad's barbecuing."

"Oh man, do I ever!"

The boys gave each other a high-five, collected the Bible, and headed into the house. It was the beginning of a great summer vacation.

5 *The Karate Kid,* 1984

Discussion Questions:

1. **What happened in the story?**

   Timmy found Jimmy standing in his garage waiting for his Bible to come alive and move.

2. **What does the Word *really* mean when it says the Word is alive and powerful?**

It means that it has the ability to change people from the inside out. It can change the way people think and therefore change the way they act.

3. How can the Word become alive in our lives?

When we read it, study it, write it, think about it and act on it, we allow the Word to change us. So by making Bible study part of our lives every day, we're inviting the Word to change us.

Notes: _____

_____

_____

_____

_____

_____

_____

_____

_____

_____

_____

_____

_____

_____

_____

_____

_____

_____

_____

_____

_____

_____

_____

_____

_____

_____

_____

_____

_____

_____

DAY 3: GIVING LESSON | THE OPEN WINDOW

Suggested Time: 10 Minutes

Offering Scripture: Bring all the tithes (the whole tenth of your income) into the storehouse, that there may be food in My house, and prove Me now by it, says the Lord of hosts, if I will not open the windows of heaven for you and pour you out a blessing, that there shall not be room enough to receive it.
—Malachi 3:10 AMPC

Supplies: ■ Single-serving-sized bags of pretzels

Lesson Instructions:

Last week, we discussed being a partner with God and what it means to tithe.

Let's review our scripture together from Malachi 3:10. It says, "Bring all the tithes (the whole tenth of your income) into the storehouse, that there may be food in My house, and prove Me now by it, says the Lord of hosts, if I will not open the windows of heaven for you and pour you out a blessing, that there shall not be room enough to receive it."

Pretty cool! Let's talk about the rewards God gives us when we listen to and obey what He shows us. He is always so good to us, and it's always a great joy to serve Him!

How about a demonstration of this scripture? Let's do that with the second part of our Offering Scripture, which says, "prove Me now by it, if I will not open the windows of heaven for you and pour you out a blessing, that there shall not be room enough to receive it." *(Ask one of the children to be your "window." Use his/her arms to form a circle.)*

Let's call this "heaven's window."

(Ask another child to hold his/her hands out in receiving position.) As the receiver, you're going to try to catch all the blessings that I'm going to send your way. *(Pour the pretzels out of the bags through the "window" opening; pouring more than your child can hold.)*

As we listen to and obey God about our giving, He'll always pour out abundant goodness on our lives!

Some rewards may come right away, and others may not. But we must trust that God is always working on our behalf, and will provide for us. He has good plans for our lives. We give our tithes and offerings because we love and honor Him, not just to receive something in return. But, the wonderful thing about God is that He loves us so much, He's always looking for ways to bless us!

God has promised those of us who choose to partner with Him, more blessings than we can hold!

And that's not all…next week we'll learn about something else He has promised. Stay tuned!

Now, let's get our offering ready for this week's service.

DAY 4: OBJECT LESSON

CHEW IT UP

 Suggested Time: 5-8 minutes

 Memory Verse: For the word of God is alive and powerful. It is sharper than the sharpest two-edged sword. —Hebrews 4:12a

Supplies: ■ 1 Banana, ■ 1 Baby bib

Prior to Lesson:

Slice the banana into small, bite-sized pieces.

Lesson Instructions:

Who likes bananas? Well, I have a nice, ripe banana for you right here! I don't want you to mess up your clothes, so we'll put this cute baby bib on you to help keep things nice and tidy. *(Present the baby bib to your child to wear during the demonstration.)*

OK, now we're ready to begin. It's time to have a slice of the banana! *(After a bite is taken, have your child stop chewing.)*

Oh, wait! One very important instruction—you'll have to eat the banana without chewing. Go for it! You can do it! We'll cheer you on! *(It will not be easy to eat the banana without chewing, so after a few tries allow the volunteer to chew and swallow the banana or discard it into the trash can.)*

You know, this is similar to how babies learn to eat. Sometimes, they put too much food in their mouths and can't chew it up. So, either they try to swallow the food whole, or they spit it out.

It's the same with God's Word. In order to get it into our hearts, we have to chew it up. This means we need to think about it, repeat it to ourselves throughout the day, and put it into action in our daily lives. When we do these things, our own words begin to reflect God's heart. We'll begin to speak words that are loving, kind and encouraging. But that transformation happens as a result of the work of God in our hearts, and the work of His Word in our lives. God's Word WILL change us, if we allow it to!

Notes: _____

_____

_____

_____

_____

_____

_____

DAY 5: GAME TIME

"NOTHING BUT NET" SWORD DRILL

 Suggested Time: 10 minutes

 Memory Verse: For the word of God is alive and powerful. It is sharper than the sharpest two-edged sword. —Hebrews 4:12a

 Teacher Tip: Present the memory verse to your children and allow them to repeat it several times. Include your own hand gestures and movements to help them remember it more easily.

Supplies: ■ 1 Laundry basket, ■ 1 Roll masking tape, ■ 1 Beach ball, ■ 2 Bibles, ■ Small prizes

Prior to Game:

Place a line of tape on the floor to designate the shooting line. The laundry basket can be elevated onto a table or placed onto the floor. Place the beach ball and Bibles by the shooting line.

Game Instructions:

This activity is a variation of a game known as a "Sword Drill." Each participant will hold a closed Bible. When a scripture reference is read, the first participant to find and read that scripture aloud can then score a point by shooting the beach ball into the laundry basket.

Game Goal:

Participants will become adept at locating and reciting scriptures from the Bible. The player with the highest score, wins!

Final Word:

God rewards those who seek Him with all their hearts. We can seek God through studying His Word, prayer (talking with Him), and by being generous and by asking Him to show us ways to bless others. God's Word is alive and teaches us how to live and love others with His heart.

Variation No. 1: Parent Play

Parents, don't miss this opportunity to play with your children. Become one of the participants, and make a meaningful memory as well as a powerful lesson.

Variation No. 2: Family vs. Family

Invite another family over for dinner, and play this game as a group. Each family can work together as a team or, 2 players, one from each family, can face off against each other during each turn.

Sword Drill Scriptures:

- **2 Timothy 3:16:** All Scripture is inspired by God and is useful to teach us what is true and to make us realize what is wrong in our lives. It corrects us when we are wrong and teaches us to do what is right.

- **Hebrews 4:12:** For the word of God is alive and powerful. It is sharper than the sharpest two-edged sword, cutting between soul and spirit, between joint and marrow. It exposes our innermost thoughts and desires.

- **Proverbs 4:20-22:** My child, pay attention to what I say. Listen carefully to my words. Don't lose sight of them. Let them penetrate deep into your heart, for they bring life to those who find them, and healing to their whole body.

- **Colossians 3:16:** Let the message about Christ, in all its richness, fill your lives. Teach and counsel each other with all the wisdom he gives. Sing psalms and hymns and spiritual songs to God with thankful hearts.

- **Proverbs 3:1-2:** My child, never forget the things I have taught you. Store my commands in your heart. If you do this, you will live many years, and your life will be satisfying.

- **Psalm 119:105:** Your word is a lamp to guide my feet and a light for my path.

- **Isaiah 40:8:** The grass withers and the flowers fade, but the word of our God stands forever.

- **John 1:1-2:** In the beginning the Word already existed. The Word was with God, and the Word was God. He existed in the beginning with God.

- **John 6:63:** The Spirit alone gives eternal life. Human effort accomplishes nothing. And the very words I have spoken to you are spirit and life.

- **John 14:21:** Those who accept my commandments and obey them are the ones who love me. And because they love me, my Father will love them. And I will love them and reveal myself to each of them.

Notes: _____

_____

_____

_____

_____

_____

_____

_____

_____

_____

ACTIVITY PAGE — UNRULY ROMAN ROADS

Memory Verse: For the word of God is alive and powerful. It is sharper than the sharpest two-edged sword. —Hebrews 4:12a

ANSWER KEY:

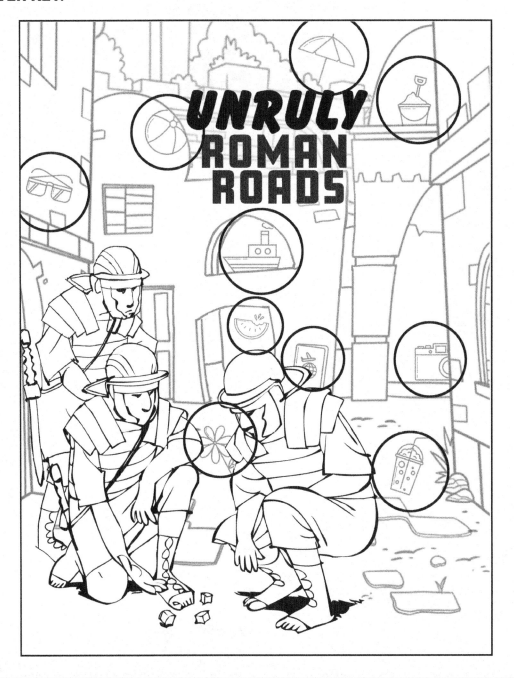

Name:_____

God's Word is powerful. It helps us to discern what is real and what is false. In this picture, look for 10 things that are false, or out of place, in this scene from ancient Rome.

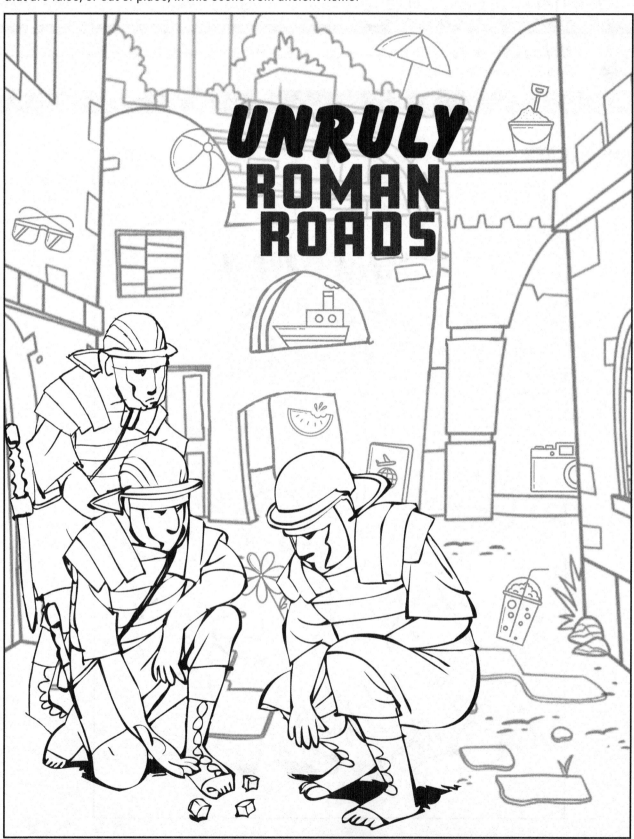

WEEK 10: IT'S SHARP AND POWERFUL

 Memory Verse: *For the word of God is alive and powerful. It is sharper than the sharpest two-edged sword, cutting between soul and spirit, between joint and marrow. It exposes our innermost thoughts and desires.*
—Hebrews 4:12

WEEK 10: SNAPSHOT — IT'S SHARP AND POWERFUL

DAY	TYPE OF LESSON	LESSON TITLE	SUPPLIES
Day 1	Bible Lesson	The Whole Armor of God	None
Day 2	Academy Lab	Is It Sharp Enough?	1 Small table, 1 8½ x 11" Sheet of paper, 1 Butter knife, 1 Plastic knife, Fingernail clippers, 1 Pair of round-nosed, paper-cutting scissors
Day 3	Giving Lesson	The Great Defender	Paper grocery bag filled with fresh produce, Small bag of wheat or oatmeal
Day 4	Object Lesson	The Right Power	1 Clay pot, 1 Small bag of potting soil, 1 Packet of seeds, 1 Hand shovel, 1 Flashlight, 1 Bottle of water
Day 5	Game Time	Power Hitter	2 Jump-ropes, 1 Whiffle ball, 1 Plastic whiffle-ball bat
Bonus	Activity Page	Armor of God Acrostic	1 Copy for each child

Lesson Introduction:

We have a sharp, exact and very powerful gift from God, which is His Word. He has given it to His children so we can be like our Father. If we can give our Superkids examples of how God uses His Word, it should help *us* realize how WE are to use His Word, as well!

Speaking God's Word will change circumstances from ungodly to godly. Applying the Word allows us to cut through obstacles and move mountains. Sharing the Word with others can bring life. Help your children see the value of God's Word and the importance of using it. It should be handled with reverence, respect and always with love!

Love,

Commander Dana

Commander Dana

Lesson Outline:

We've already learned that words are important. This week, however, your children will learn that words can be used to combat the devil and disrupt his attacks. This is a great opportunity for your children to learn how to stand up for themselves in the spirit and be powerful warriors for God.

I. THE WORD OF GOD IS POWERFUL AND SHARP

a. Speaking God's Word cuts through doubt and fear. James 1:5-6

b. Speaking God's Word brings health and life to our lives. Proverbs 4:22

c. God is never careless with His Word.

II. GOD'S WORD IS A SWORD Ephesians 6:17

a. This "Spirit Sword" in you will bring power to your prayer life.

b. This sword is wielded with our mouths, not our hands.

c. When God's Word lives in you, asking and receiving is easy! John 15:7

III. LEARNING GOD'S WORD IS AN ADVENTURE

a. God's Word has healing power. Psalm 107:20

b. Forgiveness is in God's Word. Luke 5:24

c. God's Word is encouragement for adventure. Philippians 3:14

Notes: _____

_____

_____

_____

_____

_____

_____

_____

_____

_____

_____

_____

DAY 1: BIBLE LESSON THE WHOLE ARMOR OF GOD

 Memory Verse: *For the word of God is alive and powerful. It is sharper than the sharpest two-edged sword, cutting between soul and spirit, between joint and marrow. It exposes our innermost thoughts and desires.* —Hebrews 4:12

You're teaching your children to use the Word of God. This means teaching them to seek truth in the Word, meditate on the Word so that it can change them from the inside out, and then apply the Word by putting it into practice. This discipline makes a huge difference in the life of any believer, and if your children can learn these principles now, they'll be well on their way to becoming mature, Spirit-led believers.

Read Ephesians 6:10-20:
The Whole Armor of God

A final word: Be strong in the Lord and in his mighty power. Put on all of God's armor so that you will be able to stand firm against all strategies of the devil. For we are not fighting against flesh-and-blood enemies, but against evil rulers and authorities of the unseen world, against mighty powers in this dark world, and against evil spirits in the heavenly places.

Therefore, put on every piece of God's armor so you will be able to resist the enemy in the time of evil. Then after the battle you will still be standing firm. Stand your ground, putting on the belt of truth and the body armor of God's righteousness. For shoes, put on the peace that comes from the Good News so that you will be fully prepared. In addition to all of these, hold up the shield of faith to stop the fiery arrows of the devil. Put on salvation as your helmet, and take the sword of the Spirit, which is the word of God.

Pray in the Spirit at all times and on every occasion. Stay alert and be persistent in your prayers for all believers everywhere.

And pray for me, too. Ask God to give me the right words so I can boldly explain God's mysterious plan that the Good News is for Jews and Gentiles alike. I am in chains now, still preaching this message as God's ambassador. So pray that I will keep on speaking boldly for him, as I should.

Discussion Questions:

1. **What is the armor of God?**

   The armor of God consists of the tools God gives us to resist the enemy and whatever he tries to throw at us. It is truth, righteousness, peace, faith, salvation and the Word of God.

2. **Why do we need the armor of God?**

   The enemy's mission is to steal, kill and destroy (John 10:10). If he can cause us harm, he will. Our protection against his destruction is the full armor of God.

3. **This passage also tells us to do something else. What is it and why?**

We're told to pray in the spirit at all times and on every occasion. Through Spirit-led prayer, we can be aware of the enemy's plots and know how to combat them. We can also help others through our prayers. We can pray for them to fulfill their purpose, and stand with them in the spirit as they battle the enemy's attacks.

4. **This passage refers to the Word of God as the Sword of the Spirit. What can we learn from that title?**

The Word of God is our weapon. That's how we fight the enemy.

5. **If the Word of God is our weapon, how do we use it to fight the enemy?**

Thinking purposefully on what the Bible says over and over helps us to recognize and know God's truth. We won't be enticed to believe things that are contrary to God's ways if we are focused on His Word. The Word of God also helps us combat the negative thoughts with which the enemy tries to plague our minds. When negative thoughts come, we can speak God's Word. It reminds the enemy—and ourselves—that God's Word is true, and we believe it.

Notes: _____

_____

_____

_____

_____

_____

_____

_____

_____

_____

_____

_____

_____

_____

_____

_____

_____

_____

_____

_____

DAY 2: ACADEMY LAB **IS IT SHARP ENOUGH?**

Suggested Time: 10 minutes

 Memory Verse: *For the word of God is alive and powerful. It is sharper than the sharpest two-edged sword, cutting between soul and spirit, between joint and marrow. It exposes our innermost thoughts and desires.* —Hebrews 4:12

Supplies: ☐ 1 Small table, ☐ 1 8½ x 11" Sheet of paper, ☐ 1 Butter knife, ☐ 1 Plastic knife, ☐ Fingernail clippers, ☐ 1 Pair of round-nosed, paper-cutting scissors

Prior to Lesson:

On the 8½ x 11" sheet of paper, write "POWERFUL" across the top half. On the same sheet of paper, write "DULL" across the lower half.

Lesson Instructions:

Let's review our memory verse from Hebrews 4:12, "For the word of God is alive and powerful. It is sharper than the sharpest two-edged sword, cutting between soul and spirit, between joints and marrow. It exposes our innermost thoughts and desires."

In our demonstration today, we'll be investigating the capabilities of four different tools. Some tools may look sharp, but aren't very powerful, and can only be used for a specific function.

Can anyone think of anything that is powerful and has many functions? *(Allow your children to give suggestions.)*

Those are all excellent examples! Here's one you may not have thought of: God's Word is powerful and can perform in *any* situation!

OK, let's test out the tools on this table. We'll be attempting to cut this paper in half using the various tools. *(For safety, either you, or an older child, can assist with testing out the tools on the paper. Have fun with allowing your children to test out the various tools, starting with the butter knife, then the plastic knife and next the fingernail clippers. By this time the kids will be encouraging the use of the scissors!)*

Well, all these tools look sharp, but none of them were powerful enough to cut through this sheet of paper.

How about trying the scissors? Yes! Scissors definitely accomplished the job! By using them, we were able to separate the two words on this sheet of paper: "POWERFUL" and "DULL."

Powerful words are from God and used to encourage, support and love others. Our lives are powerful when we choose to live in God's presence and ask for His wisdom and guidance.

Dull words aren't helpful to others and are used to hurt or destroy people's lives. When we choose to live without

God's presence and love in our lives, we'll be dull and unfruitful.

It took us a few tries to find the tool with enough power to cut through the paper. Remember, some tools may look sharp, but may not be very powerful at all.

Like our memory verse says, God's Word is powerful and sharp. It can cut through any doubts, fears or challenges we face. God's Word brings healing, forgiveness and hope to our lives.

Notes: _____

_____

_____

_____

_____

_____

_____

_____

_____

_____

_____

_____

_____

_____

_____

_____

_____

_____

_____

_____

_____

_____

_____

_____

_____

_____

DAY 3: GIVING LESSON | THE GREAT DEFENDER

Suggested Time: 10 minutes

Offering Scripture: For my part, I will defend you against marauders, protect your wheat fields and vegetable garden against plunderers. –Malachi 3:11 MSG

Teacher Tip: Review the previous Giving Lessons (Weeks 8-9) about being a partner with God and what it means to tithe. Allow your kids to share and discuss what tithing and being a business partner with God means to them.

Supplies: ☐ Paper grocery bag filled with fresh produce, ☐ Small bag of wheat or oatmeal

Lesson Instructions:

We become great business partners with God when we give to Him because we love and honor Him and seek His will in all we do.

Let's read our scripture together from Malachi 3:11 (MSG), "For my part, I will defend you against marauders, protect your wheat fields and vegetable garden against plunderers." *(Place the produce and bag of wheat or oatmeal on the table.)* Can anyone share what this scripture means to our lives today? *(Allow time for your children to share and express their ideas.)*

At the time this scripture was written, most people made their living as farmers. Farmers needed protection from robbers, who would steal from their crops and gardens. Today, most of us buy groceries from a grocery store!

Just like God provided protection for the farmers as they chose to sow into God's kingdom, He also protects us from harm and keeps dangerous or hurtful people from coming near us as we choose to sow into His kingdom. He will help us be responsible over everything He blesses our lives with. What a great business partner we have in God!

Let's honor God by preparing our offering for this week's service at church.

Notes: _____

_____

_____

_____

_____

_____

_____

_____

DAY 4: OBJECT LESSON | **THE RIGHT POWER**

 Suggested Time: 5-8 minutes

 Memory Verse: For the word of God is alive and powerful. It is sharper than the sharpest two-edged sword, cutting between soul and spirit, between joint and marrow. It exposes our innermost thoughts and desires. —Hebrews 4:12

 Teacher Tip: Allow your children to assist with the demonstration, and provide your assistants with the appropriate supplies/gardening tools as the demonstration is being presented to the kids.

Supplies: ☐ 1 Clay pot, ☐ 1 Small bag of potting soil, ☐ 1 Packet of seeds, ☐ 1 Hand shovel, ☐ 1 Flashlight, ☐ 1 Bottle of water

Prior to Lesson:

Place supplies onto a table for easy access. Consider placing a plastic tarp or newspaper under the project to help protect the area from any spills.

Lesson Instructions:

Today, we're going to work with some basic gardening skills. So, who would like to help me with this garden project? *(Select one of the children to assist you.)*

First, we'll add some potting soil to our clay pot. Next, we'll add a few seeds and use the shovel to cover them with more potting soil. We'll now add water to help our seeds grow. And for our final step, we'll need some light. *(Present the flashlight to the assistant.)*

Well, that should do it! Do you think anything is happening? Are the seeds growing yet? *(Allow the kids the opportunity to suggest needing "real" sunlight for the seeds to grow.)*

That's right! The seeds need "real" light to help them grow! God created the sunlight to have the right power for the seeds to grow.

Just like sunlight is the right power source to help the seeds grow, God's Word and how we use it in our everyday lives is our right source of power. There are lots of different kinds of power in the world, but the Word of God is the strongest power!

So today, make sure you go after the right kind of power. Let *God's Word* shine down and bring life to you every day!

Notes: _____

_____

_____

_____

DAY 5: GAME TIME | **POWER HITTER**

 Suggested Time: 5-10 minutes

 Memory Verse: For the word of God is alive and powerful. It is sharper than the sharpest two-edged sword, cutting between soul and spirit, between joint and marrow. It exposes our innermost thoughts and desires. —Hebrews 4:12

 Parent Tip: Present the memory verse to your children and allow them to repeat it several times. Include your own hand gestures and movements to help them remember it more easily.

Supplies: ☐ 2 Jump-ropes, ☐ 1 Whiffle ball, ☐ 1 Plastic whiffle-ball bat

Prior to Game:

It's best to play this game outdoors. Place the 2 jump-ropes on the ground in straight lines approximately 8-10 feet apart. Batters will stand on one line and the pitcher on the other, facing each other.

Game Instructions:

Let's take a moment to say our memory verse. *(Allow children time to repeat the verse.)*

Now, we're going to play a fun game that I know all of you will really enjoy! We'll need 1 pitcher who really likes baseball and would like to be first. *(Allow children to volunteer. Choose 1 pitcher for the game.)*

OK, we have our pitcher, so the rest of you will come up to bat. But, we'll play multiple rounds, so all of you will get a turn to bat and to pitch!

During each batter's turn, the batter will line up across from the pitcher, each behind his/her line, facing each other.

The pitcher will toss the ball to the batter while saying, "The Word of God is alive!"

The batter will swing at the ball and shout, "and powerful!" God's Word IS alive and powerful, isn't it? So, let's get started!

Game Goal:

This game demonstrates the "power" in God's Word and the importance of teamwork. This activity will help kids find power in speaking God's Word. The batter to hit the ball the farthest, wins!

Final Word:

Learning to recognize the power in God's Word can help us change from the inside out. God cares about our hearts and the challenges we face every day. Seeking Him, asking Him for help, and trusting in His goodness and love, helps us live in freedom.

With God, all things are possible in our lives. God has good plans prepared for us! His Word really is alive and powerful inside every boy and girl who knows Jesus!

Variation No. 1: Parent Play

Parents, don't miss this opportunity to play with your children. Become one of the participants and make a meaningful memory as well as a powerful lesson.

Variation No. 2: One Player

If you only have one player, treat this as a fun activity. Play the same but don't keep points. The player can still swing at the whiffle ball with the bat and practice proclaiming, "The Word of God is alive…and powerful!"

Variation No. 3: Beat Yourself

For children with different skill levels, or for an only child, have them play against themselves. Track how many hits each child makes in 10 pitches. Then, play another round to see whether each player can beat his/her own score.

Notes: _____

_____

_____

_____

_____

_____

_____

_____

_____

_____

_____

_____

_____

_____

_____

_____

_____

ACTIVITY PAGE   ARMOR OF GOD ACROSTIC

Memory Verse: For the word of God is alive and powerful. It is sharper than the sharpest two-edged sword, cutting between soul and spirit, between joint and marrow. It exposes our innermost thoughts and desires. —Hebrews 4:12

ANSWER KEY:

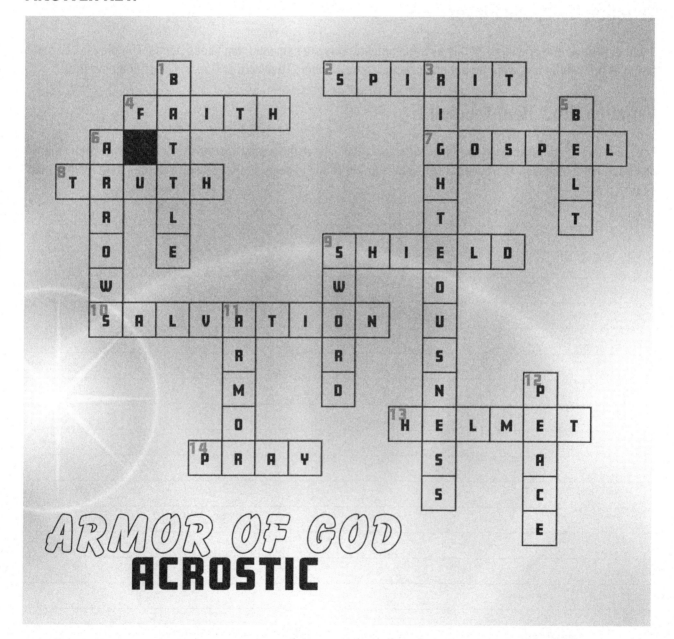

Name:_____

This week, you learned about the armor of God. It can defeat the enemy's attacks every time. Now, see if you can defeat this acrostic. Simply place the words in the given spaces. Hint: Start by filling in the longest word.

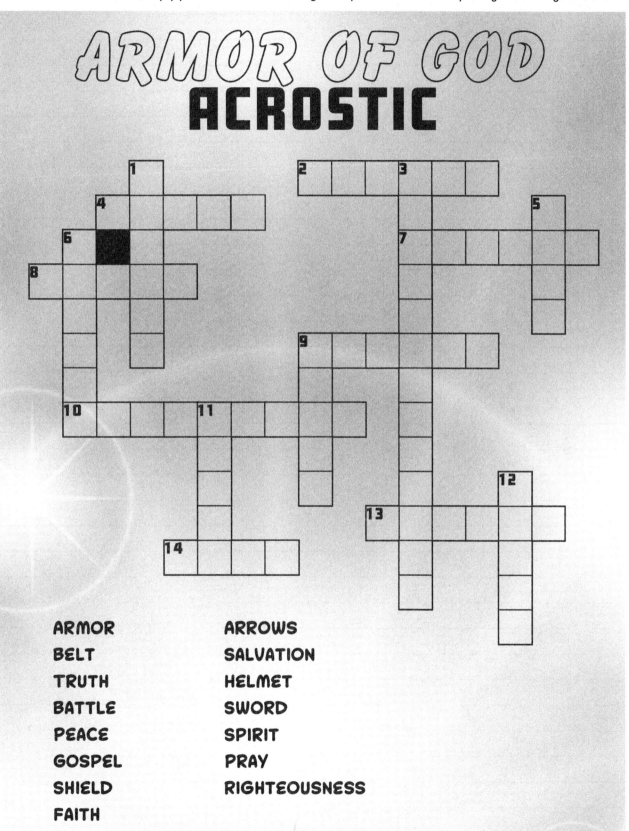

ARMOR · ARROWS

BELT · SALVATION

TRUTH · HELMET

BATTLE · SWORD

PEACE · SPIRIT

GOSPEL · PRAY

SHIELD · RIGHTEOUSNESS

FAITH

Notes: _____

_____

_____

_____

_____

_____

_____

_____

_____

_____

_____

_____

_____

_____

_____

_____

_____

_____

_____

_____

_____

_____

_____

_____

_____

_____

_____

_____

_____

_____

_____

_____

_____

_____

_____

_____

_____

_____

_____

_____

_____

_____

WEEK 11: IT'S A LIGHT!

Memory Verse: *Your word is a lamp to guide my feet and a light for my path.* —Psalm 119:105

WEEK 11: SNAPSHOT — IT'S A LIGHT!

DAY	TYPE OF LESSON	LESSON TITLE	SUPPLIES
Day 1	Bible Lesson	War With Surrounding Nations	None
Day 2	Real Deal	Thomas Edison	Pictures of Thomas Edison
Day 3	Giving Lesson	Gifts for the King	A toy camel, Various spices, Gold coins, Costume jewelry, A bag to contain your items, Small table
Day 4	Object Lesson	Darkness Is Messy	1 Large jar of mayonnaise, 1 Large package of grated cheese, Slices of bread, Plates, Blindfolds, 1 Roll of paper towels
Day 5	Game Time	Find Your Marbles	2 Blindfolds, 1 Bag of colored marbles, 1 Bag of clear marbles, 2 Small bowls for marbles, 2 Small bowls filled with water, 2 Large bowls filled with chocolate pudding, 1 Package baby wipes/towelettes
Bonus	Activity Page	Out of the Cave Maze	1 Copy for each child

Lesson Introduction:

Because God's Word is a light, and His Word lives in us, we can be a light to those around us. Because God's Word, which lives in us, is powerful, we can be powerful by speaking and sharing His goodness with others. Let's go after God's Word and walk in that light. God will show us ways to live a life of adventure through His Word and from time in His presence.

God is raising up a bright army of children to shine for Him, and you have the honor of helping your Superkids discover and live the life God has designed for them.

Love,

Commander Dana

Commander Dana

Lesson Outline:

God's Word helps guide us. It's a pivotal tool that helps us know how to live. Encourage your children to begin turning to the Word to make godly decisions. It's a discipline that will serve them well in life.

I. THE WORD OF GOD IS A LIGHT TO OUR PATH

a. God's Word helps us see clearly. Psalm 19:8

b. This light is available to all who choose to believe. John 12:46

c. It is better to walk in light than in darkness! Ephesians 5:8-9

II. KING JEHOSHAPHAT ASKED GOD FOR HELP 2 Chronicles 20

a. King Jehoshaphat and the people of Judah were being attacked. Verses 1-2

b. King Jehoshaphat needed to "see" what to do. Verse 4

c. When the Word of God came, victory came! Verse 14-17, 24

III. THE LIGHT OF GOD'S WORD SHINES ON US AND THROUGH US

a. God's light and His glory shine on us. Isaiah 60:1

b. We are a vessel for God's light. Matthew 5:16

c. God shines His light in our hearts to reveal His goodness. 2 Corinthians 4:6

Notes: _____

_____

_____

_____

_____

_____

_____

_____

_____

_____

_____

_____

DAY 1: BIBLE LESSON

WAR WITH SURROUNDING NATIONS

Memory Verse: *Your word is a lamp to guide my feet and a light for my path.* —Psalm 119:105

This week, you'll be teaching your children that God's Word is a light. It helps us see and know the truth and what is really happening around us. This is a time for your children to discover just how useful and powerful God's Word is. It *will* make a difference in their lives if they will allow it to!

Read 2 Chronicles 20:1-24:
War With Surrounding Nations

After this, the armies of the Moabites, Ammonites, and some of the Meunites declared war on Jehoshaphat. Messengers came and told Jehoshaphat, "A vast army from Edom is marching against you from beyond the Dead Sea. They are already at Hazazon-tamar." (This was another name for En-gedi.)

Jehoshaphat was terrified by this news and begged the Lord for guidance. He also ordered everyone in Judah to begin fasting. So people from all the towns of Judah came to Jerusalem to seek the Lord's help.

Jehoshaphat stood before the community of Judah and Jerusalem in front of the new courtyard at the Temple of the Lord. He prayed, "O Lord, God of our ancestors, you alone are the God who is in heaven. You are ruler of all the kingdoms of the earth. You are powerful and mighty; no one can stand against you! O our God, did you not drive out those who lived in this land when your people Israel arrived? And did you not give this land forever to the descendants of your friend Abraham? Your people settled here and built this Temple to honor your name. They said, 'Whenever we are faced with any calamity such as war, plague, or famine, we can come to stand in your presence before this Temple where your name is honored. We can cry out to you to save us, and you will hear us and rescue us.'

"And now see what the armies of Ammon, Moab, and Mount Seir are doing. You would not let our ancestors invade those nations when Israel left Egypt, so they went around them and did not destroy them. Now see how they reward us! For they have come to throw us out of your land, which you gave us as an inheritance. O our God, won't you stop them? We are powerless against this mighty army that is about to attack us. We do not know what to do, but we are looking to you for help."

As all the men of Judah stood before the Lord with their little ones, wives, and children, the Spirit of the Lord came upon one of the men standing there. His name was Jahaziel son of Zechariah, son of Benaiah, son of Jeiel, son of Mattaniah, a Levite who was a descendant of Asaph.

He said, "Listen, all you people of Judah and Jerusalem! Listen, King Jehoshaphat! This is what the Lord says: Do not be afraid! Don't be discouraged by this mighty army, for the battle is not yours, but God's. Tomorrow, march out against them. You will find them coming up through the ascent of Ziz at the end of the valley that opens into the wilderness of Jeruel. But you will not even need to fight. Take your positions; then stand still and watch the Lord's victory. He is with you, O people of Judah and Jerusalem. Do not be afraid or discouraged. Go out against them tomorrow, for the Lord is with you!"

Then King Jehoshaphat bowed low with his face to the ground. And all the people of Judah and Jerusalem did the same, worshiping the Lord. Then the Levites from the clans of Kohath and Korah stood to praise the Lord, the God of Israel, with a very loud shout.

Early the next morning the army of Judah went out into the wilderness of Tekoa. On the way Jehoshaphat stopped and said, "Listen to me, all you people of Judah and Jerusalem! Believe in the Lord your God, and you will be able to stand firm. Believe in his prophets, and you will succeed."

After consulting the people, the king appointed singers to walk ahead of the army, singing to the Lord and praising him for his holy splendor. This is what they sang:

"Give thanks to the Lord; his faithful love endures forever!"

At the very moment they began to sing and give praise, the Lord caused the armies of Ammon, Moab, and Mount Seir to start fighting among themselves. The armies of Moab and Ammon turned against their allies from Mount Seir and killed every one of them. After they had destroyed the army of Seir, they began attacking each other. So when the army of Judah arrived at the lookout point in the wilderness, all they saw were dead bodies lying on the ground as far as they could see. Not a single one of the enemy had escaped.

Discussion Questions:

1. **Tell me what happened in this passage.**

   Jehoshaphat, king of Judah, was about to be attacked. He and all his people sought the Lord for help to defeat their enemies. The Lord spoke through one of Jehoshaphat's people, the descendant of a Levite, and instructed Judah what to do. King Jehoshaphat and his people did what the Lord told them to do, and He helped them defeat their enemies.

2. **King Jehoshaphat and his people had a problem. They could have complained or given up or retreated, but instead, they did something important. What was it?**

   They turned to the Lord. They asked God for the answer to their problem.

3. **Can we do the same today? If so, how?**

   Yes, we can turn to the Lord in prayer and by reading His Word.

4. **King Jehoshaphat repeated what his ancestors had said when he said, "Whenever we are faced with any calamity such as war, plague, or famine, we can come to stand in your presence before this Temple where your name is honored. We can cry out to you to save us, and you will hear us and rescue us"(verse 9). Is that still true today?**

   Yes, the Lord still hears us and rescues us, regardless of the trouble. He will direct us if we seek Him about it. Yes, there may be consequences for our past choices, but God is gracious and He will never leave us.

5. **Do we need to go to a temple or building to hear and receive answers from God?**

   No, we can read God's Word for answers as well as talk to the Lord and listen to the Holy Spirit. Reading and memorizing the Word is so powerful because it often gives us answers before we face the problems. If we know the Word, then we'll know how to respond when problems come.

DAY 2: REAL DEAL — THOMAS EDISON

 Memory Verse: Your word is a lamp to guide my feet and a light for my path. —Psalm 119:105

 Concept: Highlighting an interesting historical place, figure or event that illustrates the theme of the day. The theme of the day is God's Word is a light to our path.

Supplies: ■ Pictures of Thomas Edison

Intro:

Today, we're talking about God's Word being a light to our path. It's true that all light comes from God, but there have been some people who learned how to harness light and make it available for the world to use. The man we'll be learning about today, spoke this famous quote, "Genius is 1 percent inspiration, and 99 percent perspiration." Have you heard this quote before? Do you know who said it? We'll learn more about this amazing inventor who certainly lived out this quote!

Today, we'll be learning about a man named Thomas Edison.

Lesson:
About Thomas Edison:

Thomas Alva Edison was born Feb. 11, 1847, in Milan, Ohio. He was one of the most important inventors in the last 1,000 years.

His inventions and work in electrical engineering have literally "lit up the world."

Thomas Edison was a daydreamer. At the age of 7, his mother began home schooling, which gave Thomas the freedom to think, learn and explore. Thomas showed talent as a businessman at the age of 7 by selling candy, newspapers and vegetables on trains to earn money.

Thomas the Inventor:

Thomas accepted his first job at the age of 19, working nights for a news company. He wanted to work nights so he'd have plenty of time to work on his inventions and experiments during the day. But one night, while experimenting at work, he accidentally spilled battery acid on his boss' desk and was fired immediately.

However, being fired wasn't such a bad thing for Thomas. After losing his job, his friend, an inventor, invited Thomas to live and work with him. This opportunity was the launching point of Thomas' career. It was here that he completed his first invention—an electric vote counter.

Building the Biggest Science Lab:

Edison had many cool ideas rolling around in his head, and most of his ideas dealt with electricity, light and sound. He dreamed of building a big science lab, with lots of inventors working for him, to help make his ideas come to life.

In 1876, Edison's dream became a reality when he sold one of his first inventions, a telegraph machine for $10,000! That was a lot of money in 1876, and is still a lot of money today, more than 140 years later.

With this money, Edison built his dream laboratory. The science lab was called Menlo Park, and it took up two whole city blocks!

A Bright Idea—The Lightbulb:

Edison wanted to invent something no one else had been able to successfully invent—a lightbulb that everyone could use.

The first lightbulbs had been developed 50 years before Edison was born, but they only lasted a few hours and were expensive to make, so no one could afford them. People all over the world still used candles to light the darkness.

Edison said he would "make electricity so cheap that only the rich [would] burn candles." The Vanderbilt family donated plenty of money to help with Thomas' experiment. *(Remember, we first heard of the Vanderbilt family when we studied about the Biltmore House in Lesson 6.)* In 1879, Thomas Edison developed his first successful lightbulb, which lasted 40 hours. This was great, but meant the lightbulb still lasted less than two days.

What if you had to change all the lightbulbs in your house every two days? Whew! Edison and his team kept working in their lab for another six months until they had complete victory. After a lot of brainstorming, more than 3,000 theories and playing with electricity, he finally did it! A lightbulb was developed that could last over 1200 hours!

Before long, people all over America were able to buy lightbulbs for their homes. This "bright" invention changed the world!

Making History:

Thomas Edison is one of the most amazing inventors of all time. Not only did he invent the everyday lightbulb and the first X-ray machine, he created over 1,093 official inventions, including the phonograph, the first movie camera, an iron-ore separator and a vote-counting machine.

Thomas Edison and his invention of the lightbulb started one of the largest companies in the world today—GE (General Electric).

Outro:

Thomas Edison brought light to homes around the world with his invention of the everyday lightbulb.

God will bring light to our paths and help us live out our big dreams and ideas. We want to partner with God and seek Him in all we think and do.

Variation No. 1: Library Trip

Schedule a trip to the library to find books on Thomas Edison and his inventions. Also, check out "The Thomas Edison Center at Menlo Park" for more online information about Thomas Edison (http://www.menloparkmuseum.org/history/thomas-edison-and-menlo-park/).

Variation No. 2: Movie Night

Schedule a family movie night with popcorn and snacks. Plan to watch one or more of the Thomas Edison documentaries on YouTube (parents, please preview) or the Public Broadcasting Service (PBS: pbs.org).

Notes: _____

_____

_____

_____

_____

_____

_____

_____

_____

_____

_____

_____

_____

_____

_____

_____

_____

_____

_____

_____

_____

_____

_____

_____

_____

_____

DAY 3: GIVING LESSON | GIFTS FOR THE KING

 Suggested Time: 10 minutes

 Offering Scripture: Bring gifts and celebrate, bow before the beauty of God, then to your knees— everyone worship! —Psalm 96:8-9 MSG

Supplies: ☐ A toy camel, ☐ Various spices, ☐ Gold coins, ☐ Costume jewelry, ☐ A bag to contain your items, ☐ Small table

Prior to Lesson:

Review the story in 1 Kings 10 about the Queen of Sheba bringing gifts to King Solomon. Display supplies on a small table, and allow your children to assist with presenting the supplies throughout the lesson.

Lesson Instructions:

Today, we'll discuss a story about a queen and a king. The queen was from a place called Sheba, and she wanted to visit and honor a famous king. This king was famous for three things: He had great wealth, immense wisdom and a desire to serve the One True God.

Can anyone tell me who this famous king is?

Yes! It's King Solomon. *(Allow the children to display supplies as each item is shared in the story.)*

The Queen of Sheba wanted to honor and show great respect to King Solomon, so she prepared many gifts for her journey.

The queen took some of her best camels. She loaded the camels with rare spices, bags of gold coins, and a lot of beautiful jewels.

All of this was to celebrate and honor a wise and rich king who was best known for serving God. Our Offering Scripture from Psalm 96:8-9 (MSG) says, "Bring gifts and celebrate, bow before the beauty of God, then to your knees—everyone worship!"

This verse describes how we are to act in the presence of a king. Just like the Queen of Sheba brought gifts to honor and celebrate King Solomon, the Bible tells us to bring gifts as an offering and expression of worship to our King—Jesus.

Let's gather our offering for this week's church service.

Variation: Something Special

The Queen of Sheba gave many special items to King Solomon. Challenge your children to give away something that is special to them. Ask them to pray about this act of worship. This is a chance for your children to give something that is meaningful as well as to recognize that Jesus is the Lord of everything in their lives—even the special things.

Notes: _____

_____

_____

_____

_____

_____

_____

_____

_____

_____

_____

_____

_____

_____

_____

_____

_____

_____

_____

_____

_____

_____

_____

_____

_____

_____

_____

_____

_____

_____

_____

DAY 4: OBJECT LESSON **DARKNESS IS MESSY**

 Time Required: 5-8 minutes

 Memory Verse: Your word is a lamp to guide my feet and a light for my path. —Psalm 119:105

Supplies: ■ 1 Large jar of mayonnaise, ■ 1 Large package of grated cheese, ■ 4 Slices of bread per person, ■ Plates, ■ Blindfolds for each child, ■ 1 Roll of paper towels

Prior to Lesson:

Arrange supplies (a plate, a scoop of mayonnaise, slices of bread, and grated cheese for each child) on the kitchen table. You may want to place paper towels under the supplies to catch any spills, or use a plastic tablecloth. This is where participants will assemble their sandwiches.

Lesson Instructions:

For the Object Lesson today, we'll be making two cheese sandwiches. Does that sound like an interesting challenge?

There's just one twist to this challenge: You'll make one of the sandwiches while you're blindfolded!

Let's begin! *(Allow your children to make the first sandwich without a blindfold and the second while wearing one.)*

OK—now you can take off your blindfolds. Let's take a look at the sandwiches. Wow—they all look very interesting, don't they? It's certainly *much* more challenging to make a "neat" cheese sandwich while wearing a blindfold! Your blindfold sandwich took a lot more time to make and is really a lot messier, isn't it?

It's the same with God's Word. Second Corinthians 4:4-6 tells us that the enemy blindfolds people, but God's spoken Word brings light into our lives and into the lives of others.

If we're blindfolded by the enemy, we're sure to make a mess of our lives, but, with God's Word, we walk in light. We are able to see the truth and make good decisions.

Second Corinthians 4:4-6 helps support this week's memory verse. Let's read and say both of these scriptures out loud, together.

As we spend time with God, we'll learn to hear His voice in our hearts. Sometimes we'll make mistakes and maybe even some messes, but God will always be there to help us and get us back on the right track when we continue seeking and following Him!

Variation: Allergy Adjustments

If food allergies are an issue, adjust the lesson by using foods that are safe for your child. Other options include:

- Cheese spread and crackers
- Chicken salad and crackers
- Peanut butter (or other nut butter) and bread (or crackers or apple slices)
- Hummus and crackers

Notes: _____

_____

_____

_____

_____

_____

_____

_____

_____

_____

_____

_____

_____

_____

_____

_____

_____

_____

_____

_____

_____

_____

_____

_____

_____

DAY 5: GAME TIME   FIND YOUR MARBLES

 Suggested Time: *10 minutes*

 Memory Verse: *Your word is a lamp to guide my feet and a light for my path.* —Psalm 119:105

 Parent Tip: *Present the memory verse to your children and allow them to repeat it several times. Include your own hand gestures and movement to help them remember it more easily.*

Supplies: ☐ 2 Blindfolds, ☐ 1 Bag of colored marbles, ☐ 1 Bag of clear marbles, ☐ 2 Small bowls for marbles, ☐ 2 Small bowls filled with water, ☐ 2 Large bowls filled with chocolate pudding, ☐ 1 Package baby wipes/towelettes

Prior to Game:

Place your supplies on the table. You may even want to play this game on a picnic table outdoors for easier cleanup!

First, mix the clear and colored marbles in 2 large bowls. Then, separate the pudding into the 2 large bowls, and cover the marbles with the chocolate pudding.

Place 2 small bowls of water next to each station for the kids to drop their chocolate-covered marbles into to be cleaned. Also place 2 more small bowls next to each station in which to place the clear marbles after they're cleaned in the water bowl. Decide in advance how many clear marbles will be found in the pudding. This will determine the winner.

Game Instructions:

Divide players into 2 teams. One teammate will wear the blindfold while the other teammate will be his/her "eyes."

When a marble is pulled out of the pudding, the teammate wearing the blindfold will place it in a bowl of water to uncover the color. If the marble is not clear, the "seeing" partner will place the colored marble back into the bowl of pudding.

Game Goal:

To uncover the clear marbles while working together as a team. The teammate without the blindfold is an example of "light" in helping their teammate know which are the clear marbles. The team that ends up with the correct number of clear marbles first, wins!

Final Word:

When we read God's Word, it becomes a guide and light for our path in this world. Let's say the memory verse together from Psalm 119:105, "Your word is a lamp to guide my feet and a light for my path."

Just like our teammate became our "eyes" for this activity, God's Word lights our way through the situations we face each day.

Variation No. 1: Parent Play

Parents, don't miss this opportunity to play with your children. Become one of the participants and make a meaningful memory as well as a powerful lesson.

Variation No. 2: One Player

If you only have 1 player, treat this as a fun activity while still making the point of treating God's Word as a guide.

Variation No. 3: Beat Yourself

For children with different skill levels or for 1 player, have the children play against themselves. Time each run to determine how many marbles each player can find in 2 minutes. Then have them try to beat that number in the same amount of time.

Notes: _____

_____

_____

_____

_____

_____

_____

_____

_____

_____

_____

_____

_____

_____

ACTIVITY PAGE

OUT OF THE CAVE MAZE

Memory Verse: Your word is a lamp to guide my feet and a light for my path. —Psalm 119:105

ANSWER KEY:

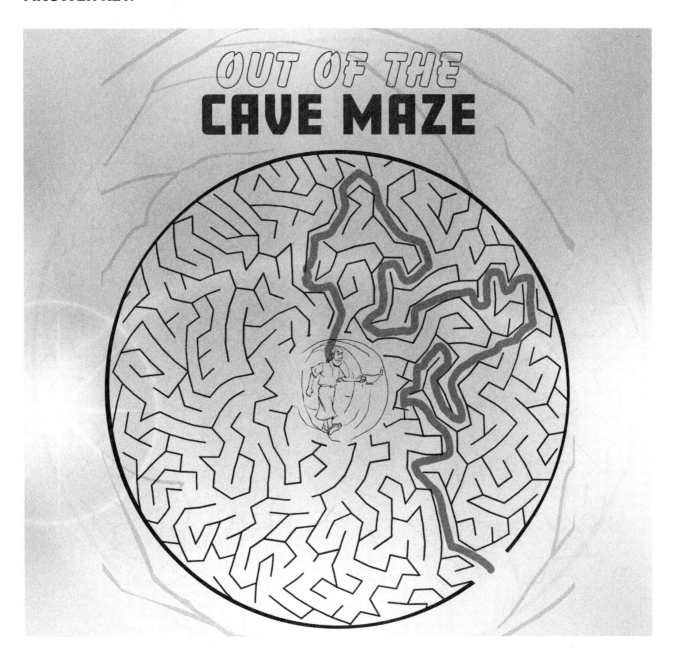

Name:_____

This week you learned that God's Word is a lamp and light for your life. It can take you out of dark places and lead you into light. Now, help this explorer find her way out of this dark cave.

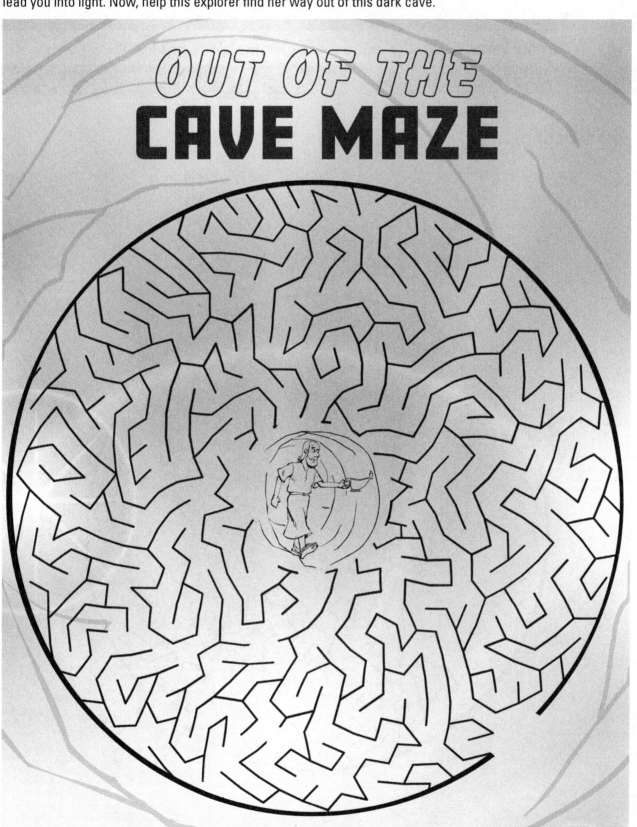

WEEK 12: WORD UP

 Memory Verse: *I have hidden your word in my heart, that I might not sin against you.* —Psalm 119:11

WEEK 12 SNAPSHOT — WORD UP

DAY	TYPE OF LESSON	LESSON TITLE	SUPPLIES
Day 1	Bible Lesson	A Call to Holy Living	None
Day 2	Read-Aloud	Timmy and Jimmy: The Stolen Bible	None
Day 3	Giving Lesson	Stay Steady	1 Jump-rope per child, Small prizes
Day 4	Object Lesson	A Safe Place	A few pieces of fake jewelry (dollar-store items), A large bill: Monopoly® game money ($50 or $100), A picture of a valuable baseball card
Day 5	Game Time	"Take Your Stand" Tug of War	1 Long rope, 1 Roll of masking tape, 1 Large sheet of poster board, Large, poster-sized cards
Bonus	Activity Page	Names of the Bible Decoded	1 copy for each Child

Lesson Introduction:

God's Word is a gift. As we read, pray and invite God into our everyday moments, we are allowing Him to shape and mold us into the people He designed us to be. We can trust in Him and His Word to be the same yesterday, today and forever. God and His Word won't pass away. We can trust that God's Word is good for us! Remember, God wants the best for our lives and He wants us to bless others!

Love,

Commander Dana

Commander Dana

Lesson Outline:

Throughout this study, we've learned about the importance of the Word of God, and this week is no different. God's Word is eternal. It never changes. It helps us live godly lives that honor Him. Your children can trust it!

I. GOD'S WORD IS VALUABLE

a. When something is valuable, we put it in a safe place.

b. We wouldn't want our most valuable treasure to get lost or stolen.

c. Our hearts are the best hiding place for God's Word! Psalm 119:11

II. GOD'S WORD, IN OUR HEARTS, HAS POWER

a. God's Word teaches us how to praise and worship. Psalm 29:2

b. God's Word will never pass away! Matthew 24:35

III. GOD'S WORD LASTS FOREVER Isaiah 40:8

a. God's Word gives us eternal life, health, peace and blessing!

b. God's Word will never pass away or lose power. 1 Peter 1:25

c. God's Word will help us love our families more, too! 1 John 4:7

Notes: _____

_____

_____

_____

_____

_____

_____

_____

_____

_____

_____

_____

DAY 1: BIBLE LESSON   A CALL TO HOLY LIVING

 Memory Verse: *I have hidden your word in my heart, that I might not sin against you.*
—Psalm 119:11

In today's Bible Lesson, you'll remind your children that they are called to live differently than other people. Because of the work that God has done in their lives, they are no longer part of the world's system. They are called to something higher, something eternal. Their salvation, and the effects of the Word of God in their lives, will stand for eternity.

Read 1 Peter 1:13-25:
A Call to Holy Living

So prepare your minds for action and exercise self-control. Put all your hope in the gracious salvation that will come to you when Jesus Christ is revealed to the world. So you must live as God's obedient children. Don't slip back into your old ways of living to satisfy your own desires. You didn't know any better then. But now you must be holy in everything you do, just as God who chose you is holy. For the Scriptures say, "You must be holy because I am holy."

And remember that the heavenly Father to whom you pray has no favorites. He will judge or reward you according to what you do. So you must live in reverent fear of him during your time here as "temporary residents." For you know that God paid a ransom to save you from the empty life you inherited from your ancestors. And it was not paid with mere gold or silver, which lose their value. It was the precious blood of Christ, the sinless, spotless Lamb of God. God chose him as your ransom long before the world began, but now in these last days he has been revealed for your sake.

Through Christ you have come to trust in God. And you have placed your faith and hope in God because he raised Christ from the dead and gave him great glory.

You were cleansed from your sins when you obeyed the truth, so now you must show sincere love to each other as brothers and sisters. Love each other deeply with all your heart.

For you have been born again, but not to a life that will quickly end. Your new life will last forever because it comes from the eternal, living word of God. As the Scriptures say,

> "People are like grass;
> their beauty is like a flower in the field.
> The grass withers and the flower fades.
> But the word of the Lord remains forever."

And that word is the Good News that was preached to you.

Discussion Questions:

1. **Tell me three things that you learned from this passage.**

   Answers will vary, but make sure your children understand the passage.

2. **What is something this Scripture passage tells us to do?**

   There are several possible answers such as we are to have self-control, live holy lives, obey God and fear the Lord.

3. **Why are we able to do this?**

   When we invite Jesus into our hearts to be our Savior and Lord, God's Holy Spirit comes to live inside our spirit. He brings with Him His love, joy, peace, patience, self-control and all the other fruit of the spirit! He makes us new creations, and His power inside us helps us to live holy lives, filled with His love, joy and power.

4. **What does the Word of God have to do with this transformation?**

   The Word of God is the power that causes faith to spring up in our hearts to receive God's promises (Romans 10:17). It's faith in Him and the power of His Word that changes us on the inside. Hebrews 1:3 says that God upholds or sustains everything by the word of His command. His words uphold, sustain and transform us!

Notes: _____

_____

_____

_____

_____

_____

_____

_____

_____

_____

_____

_____

_____

_____

_____

_____

DAY 2: READ-ALOUD

TIMMY AND JIMMY: THE STOLEN BIBLE

 Suggested Time: 10 minutes

 Memory Verse: I have hidden your word in my heart, that I might not sin against you. —Psalm 119:11

Background:

Today's story focuses on the importance of not just having or holding a Bible, but hiding God's Word in our hearts through reading, studying, confessing and believing it—then acting on it.

Story:

Timmy walked into Jimmy's bedroom one day after school to find his best friend sitting at his desk with his head in his hands. They had planned to meet after school for the Students for Christ service club meeting, but Jimmy hadn't shown up. Since he was always excited about the SFC meetings, Timmy had gone to Jimmy's house right after the meeting to make sure he was OK.

"Hey, Jimmy, I missed you today at the SFC meeting. Where'd you go?" When his friend didn't respond, he kept talking. "We talked about the booth for the school carnival. We're thinking about building a 'Dunking for Jesus' booth, and we're taking sign-ups for people to get dunked. I thought for sure you'd want to sign up." Timmy finally stopped talking when he noticed how dejected his friend looked. "Hey, what's up?" he asked.

"My locker got broken into," Jimmy said sadly.

"Get outta here! What happened?"

Jimmy lifted his head and began to talk dramatically with his hands. "I had just finished history class and went to get my lunch. We're studying the Alamo right now, which I'm still confused about since they said it was hot there. I always thought Alaska was cold."

Timmy eyed his friend suspiciously. "You know the Alamo isn't in Alaska. It's in Texas, right?"

"Then why do they have all those ice igloos?" Jimmy rolled his eyes.

"That's Eskimo, NOT Alamo!" Timmy exclaimed.

Jimmy replied, "You should be a teacher someday. You're so smart!" He was clearly in awe.

"Thanks, but can you get on with your story?"

"Oh yeah. So it was time to go to lunch, which IS my favorite class of the day," Jimmy stated.

"Lunch isn't a class."

Again, Jimmy rolled his eyes. "Says you. I think chefs would agree with me. You keep distracting me. I'm trying to tell you a story here."

"Sorry," Timmy said with a shake of his head. "Go on."

"Anyway, today is Wednesday, which means my mom sends her famous homemade, meatball sub sandwich for my lunch. It's the highlight of my school week." Jimmy jammed his fingers through his hair in frustration. "Do you even understand how *horrible* this is?"

Timmy struggled to understand what had happened. "Somebody stole your meatball sub?"

Jimmy's eyes widened. "Worse! I would have felt better knowing someone actually enjoyed the best meatball sandwich in the state. But, they didn't even eat it! They just smashed it all over my locker door and..." Jimmy stopped talking, lowered his head to his desk and began knocking it against the edge.

"And what? Where else did they smash it?" Timmy pressed.

"IN MY BIBLE!"

Timmy finally understood. "Oh man, I'm so sorry. That really stinks."

Jimmy raised his eyes to meet his friend's gaze. His desperation was clear. "I took it to lunch to read, since I didn't have anything to eat. And when I opened it up, there it was. A big chunk of a mashed-up meatball right in the middle of Psalms."

Timmy could just see it: Jimmy opening his Bible to find a big, lumpy meatball. "What a bummer," he said.

"That's not all," Jimmy continued. "It was time to go to Math class, so I picked out the chunks of meatball, which were actually still pretty tasty, and cleaned things up the best I could. But sure enough, after Math—guess what happened?"

Timmy joked, "You found a piece of garlic bread in Proverbs?"

Jimmy glared. "Ha, ha. Very funny. No, this time my Bible was stolen. Now, how am I supposed to hear from God?"

Timmy smiled. "I have good news for you. God came up with a hiding place where you could put His Word so that it could NEVER be stolen!"

Jimmy shook his head. "I'm not old enough to have my own safe."

Now it was Timmy's turn to shake his head. "Not a metal safe—it's a place that every person has where you can hide the Word—your heart."

"Come again?"

"In Psalms, God tells us to hide His Word in our hearts," Timmy explained. "You read God's Word all the time, Jimmy—so you already have God's Word hidden in your heart!"

Slowly, Jimmy began to smile as the realization of what Timmy was saying took root. "That's awesome. I forgot about that verse."

"So even if someone steals your Bible, they can't ever steal His Word from your heart!"

"Timmy, you're a great friend. Thanks," Jimmy said as he jumped to his feet. "You wanna come buy a new Bible with me? Then we can get a piece of pizza at Joe's."

"Sure. Let me ask my mom," Timmy replied. "Then maybe we can talk about who has the combination to your locker."

Jimmy nodded his head with wide eyes. "I sure don't want them getting my mom's meatball sub again, or my new Bible."

"No kidding," Timmy agreed.

The boys shared a high-five before heading out the door.

Discussion Questions:

1. **Tell me about the story.**

   Someone stole Jimmy's meatball sub and his Bible.

2. **Why was Jimmy so upset about someone stealing his Bible?**

   He thought he had lost the Word.

3. **What did Timmy tell Jimmy about the Word that gave him comfort?**

   Timmy told Jimmy that he couldn't lose the Word because it was hidden in his heart.

4. **How can we hide the Word in our hearts?**

   We can read it, memorize it, study it, confess God's promises, talk about it, share it with others and do what it says. Doing these things makes God's Word even more real and applicable to our lives. It becomes so ingrained in us that no one can steal it away!

Notes: _____

_____

_____

_____

_____

_____

_____

_____

_____

_____

_____

_____

_____

_____

_____

_____

DAY 3: GIVING LESSON | STAY STEADY

Suggested Time: 10 minutes

Offering Scripture: You have need of steadfast patience and endurance, so that you may perform and fully accomplish the will of God, and thus receive and carry away [and enjoy to the full] what is promised. —Hebrews 10:36 AMPC

Supplies: ■ 1 Jump-rope per child, ■ Small prizes

Lesson Instructions:

Who likes to jump rope? Are your jump-roping skills world-class? Let's see! *(Distribute the jump-ropes, and have your children demonstrate their skills.)*

Wow! Great job!

Since you are all expert jump ropers, let's see if you can jump…100 times! If you can jump 100 times, you'll receive a prize! *(Allow your children to count while they jump rope. If anyone misses or stumbles, continue to count where they left off for time-saving purposes.)*

Wow, that was a lot of jumping! It wouldn't be surprising if after jumping 80 or 90 times, you started thinking, *This is really hard. This takes a lot of energy. Maybe I should stop.* But you didn't. I'm impressed that you kept going and going!

Our Offering Scripture today describes *you!* Let's read it out loud together from Hebrews 10:36 AMPC: "You have need of steadfast patience and endurance, so that you may perform and fully accomplish the will of God, and thus receive and carry away [and enjoy to the full] what is promised."

You had what the Bible calls *endurance,* which means you kept on going and wouldn't give up. Do you know one reason someone might want to keep going? You're right! Because there's a prize promised!

I'm sure you're wondering about your prize! Well, before we talk about that, let me mention that this scripture shares two very important areas for us to remember: endurance and patience.

You demonstrated endurance, but now comes the patience part! We're going to exercise patience for a few hours, until after dinner, to receive your prizes. We're patient people because the Holy Spirit brought patience into our spirits when we asked Jesus to come into our hearts. I believe we can do it! *(Remember to hand out prizes after dinner!)*

Let's remember that when we pray and trust God to help us in His timing and His way, we can't give up! We must have patience and endurance as we wait on Him for answers.

Now, let's get our offerings ready for our church service.

Variation: Dessert Prize

For a prize, consider making a special dessert for after dinner.

Notes: _____

_____

_____

_____

_____

_____

_____

_____

_____

_____

_____

_____

_____

_____

_____

_____

_____

_____

_____

_____

_____

_____

_____

_____

_____

_____

DAY 4: OBJECT LESSON

A SAFE PLACE

Time Required: 10 minutes

Memory Verse: I have hidden your word in my heart, that I might not sin against you. —Psalm 119:11

Supplies: ■ A few pieces of fake jewelry (dollar-store items), ■ A large bill—Monopoly® game money ($50 or $100), ■ A picture of a valuable baseball card

Lesson Instructions:

We've been discussing an important scripture from Psalm 119:11. Let's say it out loud together: "I have hidden your word in my heart, that I might not sin against you." Can someone share what this scripture means to you? *(Allow your children to share what this means to them and how they can apply it in their everyday lives.)*

I've brought some nice jewelry, a picture of a valuable baseball card and some money to show you. If you had some nice jewelry, would you throw it around in your room—or would you keep it in a safe place? Or, if you collected baseball cards, and this particular one was a really important or valuable one, would you keep it in the bottom of your backpack?

And last of all, if you were given a real $100 bill, would you toss it on top of your dresser or leave it lying on the kitchen table?

Of course not! We want to take care of the nice things we're given and put them in a safe place. In the same way, just like our memory verse says, we want to put God's Word, which is very valuable, into our hearts so we can use it to help us make good choices every day.

We want to take care of the nice jewelry, toys or money we receive and keep them in safe places until we use them. God's Word is so important to us, we want to take some time and put it in a special place too—our hearts!

Notes: _____

_____

_____

_____

_____

_____

_____

_____

_____

DAY 5: GAME TIME | **"TAKE YOUR STAND" TUG OF WAR**

 Suggested Time: 5-7 minutes

 Memory Verse: I have hidden your word in my heart, that I might not sin against you. —Psalm 119:11

 Teacher Tip: Present the memory verse to your children and allow them to repeat it several times. Include your own hand gestures and movements to help them remember it more easily.

Supplies: ■ 1 Long rope, ■ 1 Roll of masking tape, ■ 1 Large sheet of poster board, ■ Large, poster-sized cards

Prior to Game:

Before the tug of war is played, present an object lesson. Place a masking-tape line on the floor as a line "not to cross" during the game. Lay a long rope along the floor perpendicular to the tape in a designated activity area. Prepare a list of negative situations that we can speak God's Word into for help. A few examples:

Psalm 107:20—for overcoming sickness

2 Timothy 1:7—for overcoming fear

Philippians 4:19—for overcoming poverty

Write the negative situation on the poster board for your children to easily see and read. On large, poster-sized cards, write out the scriptures you chose that can help in each negative situation. Display the poster board for your children to read and speak out while participating. Allow a parent or an older child to hold one end of the rope while your children come forward for the tug-of-war challenge.

Teacher Tip: For safety purposes, remind your children to not let go of the rope suddenly, as this could cause a fall.

Game Instructions:

Are we ready for our tug-of-war challenge? All right! One person will read one of the negative situations. At this point, our tug of war will begin. So, let's get started! *(Let one of the children compete against the adult/older child. Read the negative situation, and have the players begin pulling. The child will not win at this point. Then someone will read the corresponding scripture to fight the negative or challenging situation. When the correct corresponding scripture is read, the adult/older child will allow the child to begin winning. Allow the younger child to win as long as the correct scripture is quoted.)*

Come on! You can do it! Pull hard. Oh, I just heard one of our scriptures. Wow, it has actually strengthened you *(speaking to the child).* Look, you're winning. God is helping you to win by the power of His Word. Keep pulling. I think you're going to win! Keep pulling! *(Allow the child to pull the adult over the masking-tape line.)* You won by the power of God's Word! Way to go!

(Repeat the activity as long as time and scripture references allow. Introduce the Final Word below. Afterward, play tug of war with everyone.)

Game Goal:

The player(s) who is able to pull the opposing team over the masking-tape line, wins!

Final Word:

Challenging situations do not have to beat us. We can overcome difficulty with the Word of God. When challenging situations arise, we can speak God's Word and trust that God will help us in our times of need. God wants the best for our lives because He is so good to us and loves us so much! So let's hide His words in our hearts, and allow Him to lead and guide us. That way, when difficulties come, we'll be ready to battle them with the power of the Word of God—and win!

Notes: _____

_____

_____

_____

_____

_____

_____

_____

_____

_____

_____

_____

_____

_____

_____

_____

_____

_____

_____

_____

_____

_____

_____

ACTIVITY PAGE — NAMES OF THE BIBLE DECODED

Memory Verse: I have hidden your word in my heart, that I might not sin against you. —Psalm 119:11

ANSWER KEY:

NAMES OF THE BIBLE DECODED

THE WORD OF GOD

THE GOOD BOOK

THE HOLY SCRIPTURES

LOGOS

THE FINAL AUTHORITY

THE BOOK

GOD'S INSPIRED WORD

THE LIVING WORD

Name:_____

This week you've learned that the Word of God is eternal. It lasts forever. Below are several common names used for the Bible. Use the key to decode these names because no matter which name we use, God's Word is powerful and true!

NAMES OF THE
BIBLE DECODED

20 8 5   23 15 18 4   15 6   7 15 4

20 8 5   7 15 15 4   2 15 15 11

20 8 5   8 15 12 25   19 3 18 9 16 20 21 18 5 19

12 15 7 15 19

20 8 5   6 9 14 1 12   1 21 20 8 15 18 9 20 25

20 8 5   2 15 15 11

7 15 4'19   9 14 19 16 9 18 5 4   23 15 18 4

20 8 5   12 9 22 9 14 7   23 15 18 4

A	B	C	D	E	F	G	H	I	J	K	L	M
1	2	3	4	5	6	7	8	9	10	11	12	13

N	O	P	Q	R	S	T	U	V	W	X	Y	Z
14	15	16	17	18	19	20	21	22	23	24	25	26

Notes: _____

_____

_____

_____

_____

_____

_____

_____

_____

_____

_____

_____

_____

_____

_____

_____

_____

_____

_____

_____

_____

_____

_____

_____

_____

_____

_____

_____

_____

_____

_____

_____

_____

WEEK 13: DO IT!

Memory Verse: Don't just listen to God's word. You must do what it says. —James 1:22

WEEK 13: SNAPSHOT

DO IT!

DAY	TYPE OF LESSON	LESSON TITLE	SUPPLIES
Day 1	Bible Lesson	Parable of the Two Sons	None
Day 2	Food Fun	Messy Cooks	1 Medium-sized clear glass bowl, Serving spoons, Disposable gloves, Can opener, 2 Large cans refried beans, 2 Pints sour cream, 2 Medium-sized jars mild salsa, 1-2 Cups grated cheddar cheese, 2 Large tomatoes, 1 Bag tortilla chips, 2 Small cans of sliced black olives (optional)
Day 3	Giving Lesson	Time to Say Thanks	Teacher gifts (Ex: coffee mug, candle, gift card, apple, etc.)
Day 4	Read-Aloud	King Claw	Optional Costumes, Props, Art supplies
Day 5	Game Time	The Mystery Challenge	2 Hula hoops, 3 Different non-see-through containers, 1 Hard-boiled egg, 1 Plate, Birthday candles, 1 Bib, Toy prizes
Bonus	Activity Page	Vineyard Mix-Up	1 Copy for each child

Lesson Introduction:

This week's teaching provides an opportunity for your children to "do" and "hear." Just as God's Word gives us assignments, consider giving your children specific assignments that challenge them to follow instructions and be doers. Here are a few examples:

- Make beds for younger siblings
- Clean up the yard
- Weed the flower beds
- Clean up the garage
- Wash the car
- Make a meal for the family

Discuss other ideas with your children. Help them get excited about being doers this week. Let this translate into them becoming doers for God. Whatever they hear their heavenly Father tell them to do, they should do it quickly and without any complaint.

Love,

Commander Dana

Commander Dana

Lesson Outline:

This week, your children will learn to be hearers and doers. They will learn just how important it is to obey quickly and completely. Doing so will allow God to work through them so they can be a blessing to others and lead a rewarding life of honor and integrity.

I. HEARING IS EASIER THAN DOING

a.   It's important to be a good listener.

b.   If we don't do God's Word, we don't see who we really are. James 1:23-24

c.   God is looking for hearers and doers!

II. OBEDIENCE IS AN IMPORTANT INGREDIENT

a.   A man once asked his two sons to do some work. Matthew 21:28-31

b.   One son said he would work, and didn't. The other son obeyed.

c.   Who do you think pleased his father more?

III. GOD IS ON THE LOOKOUT 2 Chronicles 16:9

a.   Those who hear and do what God's Word says will be blessed.

b.   God has big plans and rewards for those who are hearers and doers.

c.   Consistent effort always pays off with our heavenly Father! Hebrews 11:6

Notes: _____

_____

_____

_____

_____

_____

_____

_____

_____

_____

_____

DAY 1: BIBLE LESSON — PARABLE OF THE TWO SONS

Memory Verse: Don't just listen to God's word. You must do what it says. —James 1:22

God looks for people who are quick to listen to and obey Him. The ability to do these two things is vital to living a holy, happy life. He wants people He can trust to fulfill His plans in the earth. Those plans aren't always easy, but they're important and can mean the difference between life and death.

Read Matthew 21:28-32:
Parable of the Two Sons

"But what do you think about this? A man with two sons told the older boy, 'Son, go out and work in the vineyard today.' The son answered, 'No, I won't go,' but later he changed his mind and went anyway. Then the father told the other son, 'You go,' and he said, 'Yes, sir, I will.' But he didn't go.

"Which of the two obeyed his father?"

They replied, "The first."

Then Jesus explained his meaning: "I tell you the truth, corrupt tax collectors and prostitutes will get into the Kingdom of God before you do. For John the Baptist came and showed you the right way to live, but you didn't believe him, while tax collectors and prostitutes did. And even when you saw this happening, you refused to believe him and repent of your sins."

Discussion Questions:

1. **What happened in this passage?**

   Two sons were told to go work in their father's vineyard. Only one obeyed.

2. **The first son refused to obey his father at first. Then he changed his mind. The second said he would obey, but then didn't. Which one obeyed?**

   The first son obeyed. He didn't want to obey at first, but then he did.

3. **If you were this father, which son would you call to handle something for you in the future?**

   The one who obeyed.

4. **Who do you think our heavenly Father would call to handle something for Him: someone who didn't obey last time or someone who did? Why?**

   He would call the person who had obeyed last time because He would expect that He could count on that person in the future.

Notes: _____

_____

_____

_____

_____

_____

_____

_____

_____

_____

_____

_____

_____

_____

_____

_____

_____

_____

_____

_____

_____

_____

_____

_____

_____

_____

_____

_____

_____

_____

_____

_____

_____

DAY 2: FOOD FUN

MESSY COOKS

 Suggested Time: *10 minutes*

 Memory Verse: *Don't just listen to God's word. You must do what it says.* —James 1:22

 Ingredients: ☐1 Large can refried beans, ☐1 Pint sour cream, ☐1 Medium-sized jar mild salsa, ☐1/2-1 Cup grated cheddar cheese, ☐1 Large tomato, diced, ☐1 Bag tortilla chips, ☐1 Small can sliced black olives, drained (optional)

Recipe for 6-Layer Dip

1. Start the layered dip by spreading the refried beans in the bottom of the bowl. (Be careful to not get beans on the sides of the dish.)

2. Next, using a clean spoon, place sour cream over the beans and gently spread with the back of the spoon to distribute evenly.

3. For layer 3, with another clean spoon, place salsa on top of the sour cream.

4. Sprinkle handfuls of cheese over the entire dip.

5. Top the cheese with diced tomatoes, and spread evenly.

6. Optional: Add sliced olives for the final layer of your masterpiece.

7. Grab a chip and dig in!

Supplies: ☐1 Medium-sized clear glass bowl, ☐Serving spoons, ☐Disposable gloves, ☐Can opener, ☐Ingredients for 6-Layer Dip (double recipe for lesson)

Prior to Lesson:

Prepare the dip beforehand. During the lesson, you'll prepare a sloppy version. Comparing the two will show the importance of being a good listener. Recruit your children to take turns reading the recipe. As each step is read, dump the ingredients into the bowl with no regard to the details of the instructions. When finished, the dip will look like an unappetizing mound in the bowl. Then, present the properly prepared dip at the end of the lesson for contrast, and maybe allow a little taste test! Have fun with this recipe and activity.

Lesson Instructions:

Today, we'll be making a tasty snack—a 6-layer dip! But before we get started, I'll need a good recipe reader. Who would like to help me with that? *(Choose one of the children to be your helper.)*

OK, here we go! *(As you read the recipe, construct the dip by disregarding the "fine points" of each step. This will help demonstrate what can happen when we choose to not listen and follow directions.)*

I think I'll just dump this in the container. There we go! Perfect. Now, what was the next step? *(Have the child read the next step in the recipe.)* Oh, yeah. No big deal. We'll just dump this in, too. *(After adding all the ingredients, look a little disappointed.)*

Hmm, I guess that didn't quite turn out the way it was supposed to. What do you think happened? *(Let the children tell you what they think may have happened.)*

You know, this reminds me of our memory verse today. Can anyone tell me what our memory verse says? *(Allow kids to repeat the scripture, and then have them repeat it together.)*

Yes, James 1:22 says, "Don't just listen to God's word. You must do what it says." I was listening to you as you read the recipe, but I wasn't doing exactly what you said. *(Present the properly made dip.)* This is what it looks like when we follow the recipe! Much better, isn't it?

Let's make sure we do what God's Word says. If we choose to practice living God's Word, then our lives will turn out right…like this dip! Mmmmm! Looks yummy!

Notes: _____

_____

_____

_____

_____

_____

_____

_____

_____

_____

_____

_____

_____

_____

_____

_____

_____

_____

_____

_____

_____

_____

_____

_____

DAY 3: GIVING LESSON TIME TO SAY THANKS

Suggested Time: *10 minutes*

 Offering Scripture: *Let him who receives instruction in the Word [of God] share all good things with his teacher [contributing to his support]* —Galatians 6:6 AMPC

Supplies: ☐ Teacher gifts (Ex: coffee mug, candle, gift card, apple, etc.)

Lesson Instructions:

Who knows what "Teachers' Day" is? *(Allow kids the opportunity to share and discuss.)*

Teachers' Day is one special day each year when students and parents celebrate teachers and let them know how much their hard work is appreciated. Have any of you celebrated Teachers' Day by taking a gift to your teacher?

Here are a few items kids like to give to their teachers. *(Display each item for the kids to see and share.)*

Do you know that one of Jesus' apostles, named Paul, taught people about the importance of Teachers' Day?

Let's listen to what Galatians 6:6 (AMPC) says: "Let him who receives instruction in the Word [of God] share all good things with his teacher...."

This scripture is telling us that we should celebrate and honor the people who teach us God's Word. That may be your parents, schoolteacher, children's pastor, or even your church's senior pastor. And not all gifts have to cost money. Sometimes the best gift you can give is the gift of thankfulness. Take the time to thank your teachers regularly.

Can you think of any gifts you can give that don't cost money? *(Allow your children to share their ideas.)*

We can always say thank you to our teachers. Did you know it honors God and others when we express appreciation by saying thank you? Your teachers will appreciate it, and so will God!

Notes: _____

_____

_____

_____

_____

_____

_____

_____

DAY 4: READ-ALOUD

KING CLAW

 Suggested Time: 15 minutes

 Memory Verse: *Don't just listen to God's word. You must do what it says.* —James 1:22

 Teacher Tip: This segment has many possible variations. Choose the one that best fits your family, and have fun!

 List of Characters/Costumes:
- Joe: Younger brother, farm clothes
- Bob: Stronger, older brother, farm clothes
- Mom: A hardworking mother, farm clothes
- Dad: A hardworking farmer, farm clothes

Supplies: ■ Whiteboard, chalkboard or easel with paper, ■ Dry-erase markers if using whiteboard, colored chalks if using chalkboard, or pencil (art pencils work best) and eraser, ■ Black marker and rags (to blend chalks) if using paper, ■ Art smock (to keep your artist's clothes clean)

Background:

This week's story emphasizes the importance of following directions—being obedient—and responsible. Joe and Bob didn't fully follow their dad's instructions, which could have resulted in damage to their stores of hay. But, like our heavenly Father, the boys' dad extended grace and mercy to his sons, who responded with contrite hearts.

Story:

Joe watched his brother Bob lift another bale of hay and stack it against the barn wall. Bob was 12 years old and strong for his age.

If I had his muscles, I'd be lifting a lot more hay! Joe imagined.

Their father had only given them one chore today, but it was a big one. Joe continued to relax while his older brother stacked two more bales.

"Hey, Bob, you want to go down to the creek?" Joe asked.

There was nothing Joe liked to do more than visit the creek. It was nice and cool and full of critters. A week ago Joe had spotted an enormous crawdad that had a black claw on one arm and a big, red claw on the other. Joe named him "King Claw." He was a prize that Joe fully intended to catch.

Bob picked up another hay bale and looked at Joe. "If we go to the creek, who's gonna get the rest of this hay stacked up in the barn?"

Joe loved his older brother, but thought Bob was way too responsible.

"We could go until it gets cooler outside," replied Joe. "It's way too hot right now, and besides, I think we could stack the bales a lot straighter when it's nice and cool."

His kid brother had a point. It was hot outside, but even hotter inside the barn. Besides, moving hay around was a dirty job and it made you itch—especially when hay got inside your shirt. Bob rubbed his hot, sweaty head and asked Joe, "How many bales have you stacked?"

"I don't know," Joe replied. "Maybe two or three. How many bales are left?"

"One hundred and ten, I think," Bob said.

"ONE HUNDRED AND TEN? That settles it," exclaimed Joe, "we're going to the creek!"

Just then the boys heard their mother call from the back porch. "Joe, Bob!" she hollered. It sounded funny when she did that.

"She's calling someone named Joe-Bob," said Joe with a smirk on his face.

"Glad she's not calling us," replied Bob.

Laughing, the two boys trotted toward the creek.

"Last one there's a rotten egg!" shouted Bob.

The boys ran until they reached the creek. "Now this is more like it," Joe said.

"There he is," Bob said.

Joe quickly sat up. "Who, Dad?" Joe asked.

"Not exactly Dad," replied Bob. "More like <u>craw</u>-dad! I am looking at your friend with the gargantuan claws."

"I think you're right," Joe whispered. "That's him, and he's got a big, red claw that I want!"

"What are you gonna do with him?" Bob asked.

"I don't know, make a necklace or something," answered Joe.

With one quick jump, Joe was in the water, grabbing at something under the bank. After a few splashes, Joe tossed a huge crawdad up on the bank. Both boys stared at the great, red claw.

"Wow, check that out," admired Bob.

The creature was trying to get back to the creek bank, snapping his claw shut in a threatening manner.

"No you don't," said Joe. "You get to become a necklace." Joe put his prize into an old can he had brought along.

As the boys headed back to the house, they heard a rumble in the distance.

"Sounds like thunder," said Bob. "I think we'd better high-tail it for the house!"

As they headed for the house, a black line of clouds appeared on the horizon. Lightning flashed like a giant camera, followed by a "bang" that turned into a "boom."

"Wow, that was close!" Joe exclaimed.

"I think I just felt a raindrop," Bob reported.

Joe looked at the darkening sky and thought about the 110 bales of hay located outside the barn. By the time the boys got home, rain was falling hard and they were soaked.

As the two soggy brothers walked through the back door, they came face to face with their dad.

"Hi, boys, how did the hay-stacking go?"

Bob got up his courage and stammered, "We got sorta sidetracked...."

"I noticed that when I drove in," their father answered.

Joe spoke up first, "Dad, it's my fault. Bob was working and I talked him into going to the creek."

Their father looked at his older son. "Is that right, Bob?" he asked.

"Actually, Dad, it isn't Joe's fault. It's my fault because I'm older and more responsible."

"Sit down, boys," said their dad. "Here's the deal; I want you to do the tough jobs I give you because I want to trust you just like God wants to trust us. The more He trusts us, the more He can depend on us."

"I guess we blew it," said Joe.

Both boys looked at the floor.

After a long silence, their dad spoke up. "The best thing about God is that He always gives us another chance.

"I came home early and put the rest of the hay up for you two. One hundred and ten bales, I think it was. Can I count on you boys to be dependable next time?"

"You can count on us, Dad," Bob said, as his brother nodded.

"I'm going to remember that," their father smiled. "I'm glad you had fun at the creek," he said as he walked into his bedroom and shut the door.

Joe turned to his brother, "Dad gave us grace on that one!"

"Yeah, cause we deserved something else," said Bob.

About that time a scratching sound came from the forgotten can on the porch. Joe and Bob both ran to take a look. The crawdad inside held up the red-colored claw as if to say, "What about me?" The two boys looked at one another.

"Let's let him go!" they shouted in unison.

Outside, the rain had stopped and the sun was shining again.

"Mom, Dad, we're going to the creek," they called, "that is, unless there are any chores that need to be completed first."

"Be back before dark, guys," Mom said from the kitchen. Joe and Bob ran for the creek. When they got to the bank, Joe looked into the can one last time.

"Well, King, I guess this is it. You get a break too." With that, he turned the can upside down and the giant crawdad fell into the shallows with a healthy splash.

Variation No 1:

Read the story as part of your read-aloud time. Remember: Reading the story beforehand and giving different voices to each character will help bring life to the story.

Variation No. 2:

Read the story as an old-time radio skit, complete with different actors for each part. If you are limited on participants, then have more than one part per person and change the voice. Make copies of the skit and have each actor highlight his or her lines.

Variation No. 3:

Act out the story as a fun skit. Perhaps your children can practice during the day (even creating fun costumes from everyday items) and then perform it in the evening before the whole family. Before beginning your skit, remember to introduce your cast!

Variation No. 4:

Create a storybook theater where one or more family members sketch the story on a whiteboard, chalkboard or artist's easel as another member reads the story. Initially, there will be a few supplies to purchase but don't let this be a deterrent from using the illustrated story option! Once the supplies have been purchased, they'll be long-lasting and reusable.

To make your presentation easier, lightly sketch the drawing with a pencil prior to presentation. Time may not allow the picture to be completely drawn and colored at the time of the lesson. Erase pencil lines, so light lines are visible to the artist but not visible to your children. Review the story ahead of time to determine the amount of time needed to complete the illustration while telling the story. When the story begins, use black markers to "draw" the picture, following the sketched pencil lines. Next, apply color using the pastel chalk. Then, blend the color with the rags. Finally, cut the illustration from the board, roll it up, secure it with rubber bands, and share it with one of your children!

Notes: _____

_____

_____

_____

_____

_____

_____

_____

_____

DAY 5: GAME TIME — THE MYSTERY CHALLENGE

Suggested Time: 10 minutes

Memory Verse: Don't just listen to God's word. You must do what it says. —James 1:22

Teacher Tip: Present the memory verse to your children, and allow them to repeat it several times. Include your own hand gestures and movements to help them remember it more easily.

Supplies: ☐ 2 Hula hoops, ☐ 3 Different non-see-through containers, ☐ 1 Hard-boiled egg, ☐ Plate (to put egg on during challenge), ☐ Birthday candles, ☐ 1 Bib, ☐ Toy prizes

Prior to Game:

Place the "mystery challenge" supplies into the proper containers. Label each container 1-3.

Game Instructions:

Does anyone know what it means to be brave? *(Allow your children to answer and share.)*

Someone who is brave actively faces and endures challenging situations. For today's game, I'll need players who are *brave. (Choose 2 children.)*

Let's begin with a hula-hoop contest. Whoever hula-hoops the longest will get a chance to choose a "mystery challenge" from 1 of these 3 containers. If the mystery challenge can be completed, the winner will receive a prize! If a player chooses not to complete the challenge, a prize will not be awarded, and another player may try. *(If the hula-hoop contest gets too lengthy, have the contestants work the hula-hoop down to their knees, out to their arms, etc.)*

After the hula-hoop contest, the winner may choose a challenge container. After the container is chosen, you may read the corresponding challenge out loud.

Can you guess the "mystery challenge," based on the object inside the container? *(Play 3 rounds so that players can complete all 3 mystery challenges.)*

Mystery Challenges:

Container #1	Hard-Boiled Egg	Peel the egg, and separate the shell from the white and the yolk of the egg. Keep all parts as intact as possible.
Container #2	Birthday Candles	Multiply your age times 4, and do that many jumping jacks.
Container #3	Bib	In your best little-kid voice, say, "I can eat my din-din all by myself because I'm big!" Then clap for yourself.

Game Goal:

Win the hula-hoop contest, and choose a mystery challenge. If the contestant can follow the instructions and complete the "mystery challenge," a prize will be awarded!

Final Word:

Hearing can be easier than doing. The "mystery challenges" were easy to hear, weren't they? But they weren't always easy to do. Let's be good listeners and obey what God is showing us!

Variation No. 1: Parent Play

Parents, don't miss this opportunity to play with your children. Become one of the participants and make a meaningful memory as well as a powerful lesson.

Variation No. 2: One Player

If you only have one player, treat this as a fun activity. Play the game the same way, but require that your child hula-hoops for 10-20 seconds before he/she can choose a challenge container.

Notes: _____

_____

_____

_____

_____

_____

_____

_____

_____

_____

_____

ACTIVITY PAGE

VINEYARD MIX-UP

Memory Verse: Don't just listen to God's word. You must do what it says. —James 1:22

ANSWER KEY:

Name:_____

This week's Bible Lesson shared a parable of two brothers whose father asked them to work in the vineyard. Only one brother obeyed and completed the work his father needed him to do. In the same way, God wants us to obey Him when He has something for us to do. He needs His people to listen and obey when He speaks.

Now, see how sharp your observation skills are. There are 10 differences between these nearly identical pictures. Can you identify them?

CPSIA information can be obtained
at www.ICGtesting.com
Printed in the USA
FSOW04n0510170616
21664FS